PRAISE FOR *INQUIRY MINDSET*

"Trevor and Rebecca provide incredible ideas and resources to support twenty-first-century learning! With a focus on student driven passions and pedagogy, they offer personal experiences and examples of concepts from around the globe. This book is a must-read for anyone wondering 'how can I better meet the needs of my learners?' using specific ideas, examples and tools!"

—**Brian Aspinall,** educator, TEDx speaker, and bestselling author of *Code Breaker,* Canada

"*Inquiry Mindset* is an important book on an even more important subject. Our rapidly changing world needs inquirers and lifelong learners more than ever before. With practical tips and engaging stories, Trevor MacKenzie and Rebecca Bathurst-Hunt offer a blueprint for how to inspire and guide inquiry-based learning."

—**Warren Berger,** author of *A More Beautiful Question,* USA

"Trevor MacKenzie expands on his first book with another powerful argument for inquiry-based learning by challenging educators to stoke students' curiosities, hear their voices, and nurture their hearts. *Inquiry Mindset* provides practical advice, examples, strategies, and resources for teachers, so they can meet those challenges for their own professional learning. MacKenzie takes readers on their own personal journeys to discover how they can become inquiry teachers. I highly recommend *Inquiry Mindset* for any teacher who wants to harness the potential for increasing student agency over learning."

—**Barbara Bray,** author of *Make Learning Personal* and *How to Personalize Learning,* host of *Conversations on Learning* podcast, and education consultant at Rethinking Learning, USA

"What a gift Trevor MacKenzie and Rebecca Bathurst-Hunt bring with their new book, *Inquiry Mindset*! This comprehensive guide supports teachers at every level, from understanding the research and theoretical base for inquiry, to managing the smallest details, including classroom setup, developing research questions, and leading kids through a gradual-release model of authentic investigations. The authors like to offer what they call *provocations*, an experience designed to 'stir thought, wonder, engagement, curiosity, and questions with our learners.' Read *Inquiry Mindset*, you will be delightfully provoked."

—Harvey "Smokey" Daniels, author of
The Curious Classroom, USA

"In MacKenzie's follow-up to the highly acclaimed inquiry resource *Dive into Inquiry*, he brings his philosophy on learning (and teaching) to life in *Inquiry Mindset*. Nebulous educational goals such as *personalized learning* and *embracing voice and choice* are brought to life through an enchanting narrative, brimming with a perfect blend of idealism and applicability. Each chapter is full of anecdotes, resources and sketchnotes that will resonate deeply with the reader, helping educators gain the tools and understandings to accomplish that which we value most in education—honouring each student as highly unique individuals with their own passions, talents and curiosities just waiting to be nurtured and explored more meaningfully in the classroom. Get your copy of *Inquiry Mindset* today . . . you won't be disappointed!"

—Sylvia Duckworth, EdTech consultant, author of
Sketchnotes for Educators, Canada

"Bringing meaning into the halls of our schools, relevance into our classrooms, and authenticity to our students' learning are all at the forefront of the educational transformation we are witnessing around the globe. After reading Trevor MacKenzie and Rebecca Bathurst-Hunt's superb *Inquiry Mindset*, I knew we were kindred edu-spirits. This book is brimming with inspiring steps to empowering our students. It's a book that needs to be read!"

—**Amy Fast,** assistant principal, author of
It's the Mission, Not the Mandates, USA

"*Inquiry Mindset* validates who I am as a teacher and illustrates the way for me to become the teacher I really want to be. This book has it all: the what, why, and how to bring the inquiry model of teaching into your classroom. The authors invite you to examine your own practices, provide concrete solutions to elevate your craft, and even share practical ways to bring curiosity and wonder into your students' lives!"

—**Lisa Highfill,** teacher, tech integration coach, and
coauthor of *The HyperDoc Handbook*, USA

"Are you a lifelong learner and want the same for your students? Changing your classroom culture is about providing the environment where students can inquire—and find answers to—what THEY want to know. *Inquiry Mindset* provides scaffolds for what many elementary educators long for, along with myriad resources, stories, and examples educators can use to help create authentic learning opportunities that foster a culture of inquiry. If we use these scaffolds, all the way up through free inquiry, we can facilitate moments memorable enough to develop lifelong learners in our schools."

—**Joy Kirr,** author of *Shift This* and brave educator
of middle school students, USA

"*Inquiry Mindset* is a practical guide to bringing inquiry into your classroom. Filled with ideas to help you ask great questions and develop curiosity in your students, *Inquiry Mindset* will help you create a learning environment that inspires students to truly fall in love with learning."

— Aaron Hogan, author of
Shattering the Perfect Teacher Myth, USA

"If you loved *Dive into Inquiry*, you'll go bananas for *Inquiry Mindset*! If you've yet to discover Trevor MacKenzie's work, you're in for a real treat! This is the perfect book to push your instruction and set you (and your students) up for student-driven learning."

—Jennie Magiera, author of *Courageous Edventures*, USA

"*Inquiry Mindset* offers practical and proven advice for bringing the goals of 'genuine student inquiry' and 'personalized learning' to life in your classroom. A rich narrative weaving accessible inquiry processes with achievable outcomes, *Inquiry Mindset* is a must-read for educators."

—Jay McTighe, coauthor of the
Understanding by Design® series, USA

"'What job do you want? No, what change do you want to make in the world?' If this is your focus in education, Trevor and Rebecca have provided an inquiry handbook bursting with examples and thoughtful processes. *Inquiry Mindset* leaves behind the do-whatever-you-want approach to inquiry and offers a concrete roadmap you can follow to success—including stops along the way for wonderings! This book will help your classroom change to keep up with the world's demanding requirements of our students."

—Matt Miller, author/blogger of *Ditch That Textbook*,
speaker, 10+ year classroom veteran, USA

"If you truly want to develop an inquisitive classroom culture that is powered by your students' curiosity, a classroom where no student is afraid to sit in the driver's seat of their learning and poke at it, explore it and ask questions, then *Inquiry Mindset* is for you. *Inquiry Mindset* will provide you with practical tips and ideas that will support you to develop your understanding of and approach to inquiry-based learning so that your students become comfortable with turning their learning inside out. MacKenzie and Bathurst-Hunt provide invaluable insight into the inquiry-cycle, the types of student inquiry, the four pillars of inquiry and the role of questions in the inquiry process. As Albert Einstein once said, 'The mind that opens to a new idea never returns to its original size,' and this is very true of the *Inquiry Mindset.*"

—**Kathryn Morgan,** director of CPD and
Research Based Learning at the Prince Albert
Community Trust, Birmingham, England

"The power of student curiosity and inquiry in the classroom is boundless and when teachers embrace student questions and recognize these as starting points to learning, inevitably amazing things happen. But how do we harness the wonderings and imaginations of our learners? How do we foster a culture that celebrates curiosity? *Inquiry Mindset* demystifies what this looks like for teachers in their classrooms and provides educators with the understanding necessary to truly empower students. A touching narrative, bursting with inspiring yet practical ways to honour student curiosities, *Inquiry Mindset* will transform your teaching!"

—**Ramsey Musallam,** EdD, high school science teacher
and author of *Spark Learning*, USA

"*Inquiry Mindset* is a book that says quite clearly we cannot just hope that 'inquiry happens.' Instead, it's important to deliberately foster an *inquiry mindset* in the classroom. Once that commitment is made, there are many ways to make sure that 'inquiry happens.' The authors' passion for student engagement shines through in every chapter as they provide a plethora of familiar, as well as innovative, tools and methods that can help foster inquiry in any classroom. Ultimately, this can lead to the most important outcome; genuine self-directed learning."

—Dan Rothstein, author of *Make Just One Change*, USA

"Trevor MacKenzie has followed up on the highly popular *Dive into Inquiry* with another inspiring journey into personalized learning with *Inquiry Mindset*. This book is full of practical and insightful steps to bring inquiry-based learning into your classrooms. Each chapter offers actionable ideas that will inspire, inform, and bring meaningful change for your students. *Inquiry Mindset* needs to be in the hands of today's teacher who wants to move from the old—to the relevant!"

—Don Wettrick, author, *Pure Genius: Building a Culture of Innovation*, CEO, StartEdUp, USA

"In this practical and powerful follow up to the well-received *Dive into Inquiry*, MacKenzie and Bathurst-Hunt share how to engage students in a cycle of inquiry. They offer classroom strategies and case studies to show how to strike a balance between expected curricular outcomes and growing students' capacity to generate and pursue curiosities. This is the hallmark of personalized learning as we grow students through gradual release of responsibility as well as provide both structure and freedom to keep free inquiry feasible."

—Allison Zmuda, author and education consultant, USA

TREVOR MACKENZIE
WITH REBECCA BATHURST-HUNT

INQUIRY
MINDSET

NURTURING THE DREAMS,
WONDERS, & CURIOSITIES OF
OUR YOUNGEST LEARNERS

Inquiry Mindset
©2018 by Trevor MacKenzie with Rebecca Bathurst-Hunt

For information regarding permission, contact
the publisher at info@elevatebooksedu.com.

These books are available at special discounts when purchased in quantity for use as premiums, promotions, fundraising and educational use.

For inquiries and details, contact the publisher:
info@elevatebooksedu.com.

Published by ElevateBooksEdu
Editing and Interior Design by My Writers' Connection
Cover design by Genesis Kohler
Author photo by Sherri Martin

Library of Congress Control Number: 2018933312
Paperback ISBN: 978-1-7336468-4-0
eBook ISBN: 978-1-7336468-3-3
First Printing: February 2018

DEDICATION

TO OUR MOTHERS,
FOR HELPING US DREAM BIG DREAMS,
FOLLOW THROUGH ON OUR PASSIONS,
AND FOR LOVING US UNCONDITIONALLY.

CONTENTS

FOREWORD

The publication of Carol Dweck's phenomenal book *Mindset* not only helped challenge and deepen our understanding of the nature of learning but also contributed a powerful term to the contemporary lexicon of teaching. We are now so much more aware of the impact of the *mindset* we bring to the classroom. The assumptions and beliefs we have about our roles, about the purpose of school, about students, and about learning itself determine what we do and say. Our mindset matters. In turn, what we do and say has a significant impact on the mindsets of our students. Amongst other things, our design of classroom spaces, the kinds of questions we ask, the degree of choice and voice we afford our learners, the nature of our collaboration with other teachers, and our use of digital tools combine to influence the way our students see learning and see *themselves* as learners.

For more than thirty years, I have advocated the use of an inquiry approach to learning. The contemporary work in this field stands on the shoulders of giants. From Socrates to the seminal work of Dewey, Bruner, Vygotsky, Freire, and others who challenged notions of the learner as a passive recipient of information instead describing learning as an active process of *construction* by the learner. In essence, inquiry is the manifestation of this constructivist view. It has a long and rich history and many champions, but the challenge remains in many schools to shift *mindsets* and to prize away the vice-like grip of conservative perceptions of what it means to teach and learn.

Through years of work in classrooms, I have come to understand that which now seems blindingly obvious. For students to truly inquire with depth, tenacity, and joy—they need teachers who, themselves, are inquirers. They need teachers who bring an inquiry mindset to the classroom.

It is abundantly clear from reading this book (and its predecessor *Dive into Inquiry*) that Trevor MacKenzie is one such teacher—a teacher who is passionate about giving students every opportunity to follow their passions and to develop the skills and dispositions so important to a rapidly changing landscape of both learning and living.

Rethinking our work as teachers takes time and effort. The simple, accessible guidance that this book contains provides the kind of practical support needed for teachers to make change. The enthusiasm Trevor and his coauthor, Rebecca Bathurst-Hunt have for their subject bounces off the pages, particularly in the sharing of their own experiences or through the many delightful vignettes of teachers implementing aspects of the approach. These examples are real, rich, and relatable. Fresh ways of interpreting and describing what it means to be an inquiry teacher, how to structure an inquiry journey, how to help kids follow their passions, and the role of the teacher librarian in an inquiry context make *Inquiry Mindset* an engaging read and a welcome addition to the field. Trevor and Rebecca are careful to reiterate what has long been understood about effective inquiry: that it doesn't just happen—it requires careful thought, planning, and scaffolding by both teachers and learners.

This book opens with a personal reflection on the insights Trevor gained watching his first child grow. Like so many parents, he longs for an educational experience that will truly value the unique "characteristics, needs, and interests" of his son. By making their own experience with inquiry available to other teachers through this book, Trevor and Rebecca have gone a long way to honouring that principle. Reading through these pages is indeed heartening. The inquiry work pioneered so long ago remains in good hands as a new generation of educators discovers the power of an approach that truly places the learner at the centre.

Kath Murdoch
author, *The Power of Inquiry*

DEFINITIONS

Inquiry is the dynamic process of being open to wonder and puzzlements and coming to know and understand the world.

—Alberta Focus on Inquiry, 2004

Inquiry-based learning is a process where students are involved in their learning, create essential questions, investigate widely, and then build new understandings, meanings, and knowledge. That knowledge is new to the students and may be used to answer their essential question, to develop a solution, or to support a position or point of view. The knowledge is usually presented to others in some sort of a public manner and may result in some sort of action.

—Alberta Focus on Inquiry, 2004

Types of Student Inquiry is a scaffolded approach to inquiry in the classroom, one that gradually increases student agency over learning while providing learners with the necessary skills, knowledge, and understanding to be successful in their inquiry.

PREFACE

When my (Trevor's) first son, Ewan, was born, my role in the classroom, my philosophy on learning, and my understanding of what it means to be an educator all changed— for the better. In truth, Ewan and my experiences with him are the inspiration for *Inquiry Mindset* and my approach to teaching.

Ewan has always been exceptionally curious, verbal, and empathetic. My wife and I watched these unique characteristics surface as soon as he began making sense of the world around him. As a toddler, Ewan loved to make up stories while he looked at picture books. He created fantasy worlds that transcended into reality and dripped into all aspects of our lives. A hike in the woods turned into an exquisite adventure. A trip to the grocery store became a scavenger hunt. He used toy blocks to construct a world full of fictional beings and mythical creatures.

Ewan put words to experiences and memories, exhibiting a vocabulary beyond his age. Perhaps most significantly, Ewan *felt* things. When a preschool classmate was absent, Ewan showed concern for the student's wellbeing. When a lively song played on the radio, he danced. When a book character hurt, he hurt too. Beyond simply being a sensitive child, Ewan has always led with his heart.

My wife, Sarah, and I have always loved Ewan's endless curiosity, his magical way with words, and his open heart, and we have actively tried to honour these important personality traits through the way we parent. By encouraging him to explore his interests through books, cartoons, games, and imaginative play, we have always aimed to nurture the spirit *within* our son. Perhaps that's why we were so anxious about him entering kindergarten. We wondered ...

Would our educational system meet his needs and honour the characteristics we loved in our son?

Would his teachers spark his curiosities?

Would they hear his voice?

Would they nurture his empathy?

The closer Ewan got to starting school, the more anxious and concerned we became. We wanted his personality to be honoured, supported, and celebrated. We wanted his teachers to truly *know* our son and to be able to describe to us at Parent–Teacher Night the traits we had grown to cherish during his young life.

As a high school teacher, I have witnessed the negative impact that overprescribed learning objectives and standardized curricula and assessment tools have on students like Ewan. Somewhere in their *schooling*, students become less curious, less adventurous, and less in love with learning. Sarah and I didn't want Ewan to experience this sort of depersonalization in his education. With that in mind, we were prepared to take action to ensure that this didn't happen to our son.

Did we arrange a sit-down with his teacher and ask what she would do to best meet Ewan's needs?

No.

Did we phone the principal and request that Ewan be assigned to a class with a teacher who would be more understanding of our concerns?

Nope.

Did we enroll Ewan into a private school with smaller class sizes?

Not a chance.

I did something even *more* drastic.

I took a good hard look at my own teaching practices. I decided to look at the unique characteristics, needs, and interests of each of my learners just as I did with my own son. With this mindset—seeing all my students as unique in their own special ways—I determined to honour them in my classroom. As a result, they helped shape my role as their teacher.

As Ewan entered kindergarten in September, ready to tackle the world and learn great things, I examined my classes through a new lens on teaching and a revised outlook on being an educator. I determined that, if I were to be the kind of teacher I'd want my son to have, I needed to leave behind everything I thought about teaching and start anew. On the first day of school, I fundamentally changed my role in the classroom. Instead of distributing a course syllabus, my customary first-day routine, I challenged my seniors to help me co-design our English course by sharing topics they wanted to discuss, problems they wanted to solve, and ways they wanted to demonstrate their understanding. My hope was to make our class a place where their voices were celebrated and their passions, interests, and curiosities were honoured. Accomplishing these goals required that my students take on a more active, meaningful, and personalized role in their learning.

It took several days, but we co-designed a course syllabus that was uniquely *ours*. We shared ideas, advocated for our learning needs, and discussed different ways of demonstrating understanding—alternatives to more traditional assignments usually evident in classrooms. These first few days were perhaps the most challenging of my career. Releasing control and power in the classroom and finding comfort in the mess of uncertainty was incredibly challenging for me. My students also struggled during these days. They had a preconceived notion of how the class would operate, and I had flipped the course structure on its head.

Despite a bumpy start, the process yielded great benefits. Not only did we create mutual ownership of the course, but through this ownership, we also built trust that allowed us to begin an exceptionally meaningful learning journey together. During the coming weeks and months, I witnessed the amazing writing and collaboration one would expect of a senior-level English class. But what I found even more valuable was the power of the trust and ownership we had built, which was reflected in the original, authentic work my students created. Here's a small sample of the personalized way they demonstrated their learning:

- a collection of paintings representing character changes across a novel series
- a choreographed dance piece representing theme in a collection of poetry a student had read
- a public service announcement educating viewers about different sexualities and romantic orientations
- a welded sheet metal dragon depicting symbolism in a novel
- a student-created video game reflecting the central conflict and plot of a historical fiction novel
- a 140-page novella about a young and impressionable teen desperate to fit into her high school social scene

Time after time, my students surprised me with their work. They had a voice in the direction of our course, and as a result, they cared about what they were learning. Throughout the year, we discovered a sense of ownership, trust, and authenticity that empowered us to reconnect with an inner curiosity we hadn't felt in a long time. We each rekindled a passion for learning—something our educational experience had deprived us of for a number of years. The experience was quite emotional for all of us, and my teaching hasn't been the same since.

Inquiry Mindset is about empowering our learners with the tools, understanding, and skills to make a difference in the world. The ideas Rebecca and I share here will clarify the inquiry process, how we use it in our classrooms, and what our learners gain from it throughout the year. We know that if you apply the philosophy of *Inquiry Mindset* to your classroom, the learning experiences, wonderings, and provocations will truly transform your teaching and forever change your students' view of what education can and should be.

> " *Inquiry Mindset* is about empowering our learners with the tools, understanding, and skills to make a difference in the world. "

With this in mind, I have a challenge for you:

As you read this book, keep Ewan in mind. Consider how he would respond to our proposals. Imagine him in our inquiry classroom and consider whether his curiosities, voice, and heart would be honoured. As you return to your classroom, look at your students through a different lens. See them like my son, Ewan: uniquely special in their own ways. If you're able to see your students in this manner, the things that muddy the waters of our profession—the overprescription and standardization that fails to honour the joy of learning innate to each student—will become a little less important. Choose to stoke students' curiosities, hear their voices, and nurture their hearts. I have no doubt that, if we are all able to do this, the futures of our learners—and of Ewan—are in good hands.

Thank you.

Trevor

HOW TO USE #INQUIRYMINDSET IN ACTION

At the end of each chapter of *Inquiry Mindset*, you'll discover prompts we have termed *#InquiryMindset in Action*. These short and powerful calls to action will ask you to reflect on your reading and put some of what we propose **into action**. Once you've done so, we ask that you capture and share these actions items with our *#InquiryMindset* community by tweeting them out, sharing them with your Instagram friends, and posting them in your Facebook groups. **In inquiry, we are all better together**. With this in mind, let's all commit to sharing our learning as we read so we can collectively support one another in becoming the teachers our students need. Enjoy!

THE INQUIRY TEACHER

Teachers are the single greatest factor in ensuring a successful transition from traditional pedagogy to the adoption of inquiry in our classrooms. Beyond leadership and school culture, resource support and collaboration with colleagues, and the design of our spaces, a successful inquiry classroom depends on teachers working with students *in inquiry*. Both *Inquiry Mindset* and *Dive into Inquiry* aim to support teachers in their endeavour to integrate inquiry in every classroom. Whilst being fulltime inquiry teachers in the classroom (Rebecca in kindergarten and Trevor in high school), we are also inquiry coaches. We spend a considerable amount of time supporting teachers, schools, and districts in their adoption of an inquiry approach to learning. It is through this lens, through our coaching, consulting, sharing, and teaching, that we've created *Inquiry Mindset*. We will provide richly authentic examples of inquiry in practice and share successful strategies and structures for allowing learners to adapt to their ever-changing roles in learning. These books pave the way for inquiry to truly amplify learning and empower student voice.

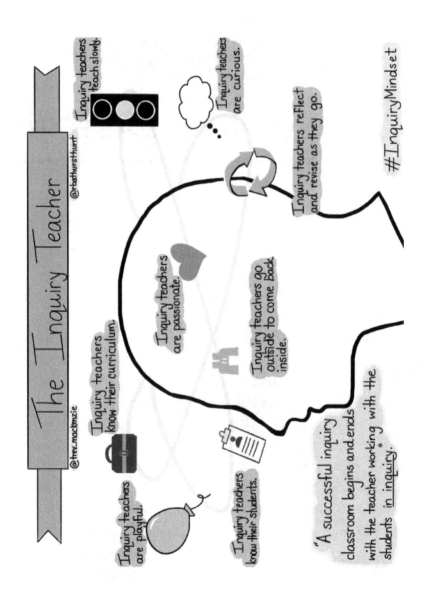

The resources presented in these books, however, will only work when you, the teacher, possess the specific characteristics that empower you to harness the potential of increasing student agency over learning. The good news is that, wherever you are in your teaching career, these characteristics can be learned, nurtured, and honed. Through consistent and intentional use, they can become part of your teacher DNA. And as you cultivate these essential characteristics, you will become the inquiry teacher that your students need you to be.

To assist you in your learning journey, we want to demystify the characteristics of the inquiry teacher. We want to clarify the nuances inquiry teachers demonstrate, the savviness they possess, and the mindset they embody. As we discuss these characteristics, reflect on your teaching practice. Which of these characteristics do you already possess? Which ones are you working to sharpen? Which ones do you need to add to your repertoire?

INQUIRY TEACHERS ARE PLAYFUL

Inquiry teachers playfully approach their practice. They find joy in learning and doing, and they share their delight with others. As a result, they cultivate a natural love of learning in their students. Their practice is grounded in playful pedagogy—the act of finding joy in being reflective and growth-focused in their teaching. This playfulness seeps into all they do, impacting the attitudes they model to their students even when facing obstacles. They see challenges as opportunities to tinker in their practice and look at problems from different angles.

INQUIRY TEACHERS TEACH SLOWLY

Inquiry teachers don't get bogged down with coverage or content. Rather, they focus on slowing down learning to allow opportunities to deepen understanding, better support their students, and embrace the curiosities, passions, and interests of their learners. Learning is not a checklist of objectives or content-specific aims. Learning is a *process* demanding time for rich and meaningful reflection; it cannot be bound or confined to bell schedules and class periods. Inquiry teachers recognize this and embrace a slower pace in their practice, taking time to observe and letting these observations guide their teaching. Likewise, they help learners take time to observe their own feelings, emotions, successes, and challenges in their learning.

INQUIRY TEACHERS KNOW THEIR CURRICULUM

Inquiry teachers are intensely familiar with what they'd like their learners to know. Their deep understanding of the content and curriculum and predetermined destination of learning provides inquiry teachers with a certain creative freedom in their practice. They are creative in the pathways they take to learning, the learning experiences they foster, how they cultivate learning opportunities for their students, and how they weave student curiosities into their classroom. A deep understanding of their curriculum serves as the foundation to pursuing inquiry with their students.

INQUIRY TEACHERS KNOW THEIR STUDENTS

Inquiry teachers know their students' stories, passions, interests, and goals, and they use this knowledge to empower learners.

They help their students understand learning and identify their own learning needs. Inquiry teachers ask students questions about themselves so the teacher and the student can learn more about the *whole child*. Inquiry teachers construct learning moments calling for reflection and sharing of self. These opportunities connect the learning to their lives, establishing relevance and authenticity. Inquiry teachers actively plan and work toward building relationship and trust, the backbone of sharing in meaningful learning throughout the year. The inquiry teacher helps learners connect their stories, passions, interests, and goals to the curriculum, shaping learning moments and direction.

INQUIRY TEACHERS REFLECT AND REVISE AS THEY GO

Inquiry teachers have a knack for reflecting and revising to better meet the needs of their students. During learning, inquiry teachers are highly aware of what's happening around them. They take time to stop and listen; they view their learners as collaborators they can learn from to better move forward. They pick up on the slightest clues and use these to shape their next steps. Inquiry teachers also reflect on their own role in the classroom, constantly asking themselves questions to guide their practice and inform their decisions. They reflect on their own actions, words, thoughts, and feelings, using these cumulative reflections to revise their path to better meet the needs of their students.

INQUIRY TEACHERS GO OUTSIDE TO COME BACK INSIDE

Inquiry teachers look beyond their classrooms for learning opportunities for both their students and themselves. Understanding that learning often occurs outside the classroom, they look to their community for connections to learning and their curriculum and identify partnerships and collaborations to create rich learning experiences and opportunities to deepen understanding. They don't see limitations or barriers keeping them from these partnerships; they dream big and take action to achieve their dreams. Looking beyond their own building to impact their professional development, they participate in inspiring PLNs (professional learning networks) and are often involved in collaborative inquiry guiding their practice. By seeking learning outside their own classrooms, they return better equipped for inquiry.

INQUIRY TEACHERS ARE CURIOUS

Inquiry teachers are inquirers themselves. Curiosity is at the heart of what they do, and they daily demonstrate and put voice to their own wonderings for their students to see. They are inquisitive and invite their learners to ask questions and explore. They cultivate their students' curiosity through provocations and wonderings, modeling how inquisitive questions can drive learning opportunities. In inquiry classrooms, questions spiral to shape lessons, direct instruction, and encourage critical thinking and revision, which leads to even deeper questions.

Students need to see their teachers as learners. They need to see teachers ask big questions of themselves and try on new things. They want to see teachers who are passionate about kids and excited about learning.

INQUIRY TEACHERS ARE PASSIONATE

Inquiry teachers love the classroom. They are passionate about kids and excited about learning. Their infectious energy ignites a passion for learning in their students, colleagues, and leaders. Inquiry teachers are not merely cheerleaders of content; rather, their genuine love for learning and the understandings they foster in their practice have an immensely positive impact on their classroom. They personify lifelong learning and, as such, their students' experiences help them create a future vision of their own learning. Their passion for learning is unwavering and is evident in many ways: their care for planning learning experiences, their tact in building relationships in their classroom, or their expertise in fostering wonderings. Underlying all of these is an authentic joy and love for their learners and their work.

You have embarked on this inquiry journey with us because you believe in the impact of providing agency over learning. You believe our educational structures need a more personalized approach, and the fact that you're reading this book tells us that you're willing to take some risks to undertake the professional growth necessary to ensure that you successfully adopt inquiry.

With those goals in mind, we encourage you to reflect on the characteristics of an inquiry teacher and on your teaching and the type of classroom you currently have by using our Inquiry Teacher: Elevate Your Mindset reflection. Take a moment to consider which of these characteristics you already possess, which you're working toward sharpening, and which you need to add to your repertoire. Think about each of the prompts and answer with more than a simple *yes* or *no*. Reflect on how these characteristics surface in your teaching. Be explicit about how you demonstrate these behaviours daily in your practice. Rate yourself on a scale: Where do you currently land between inquiry *novice* and inquiry *master*?

Inquiry Teachers Are Playful
NOVICE ← 1 2 3 4 5 → MASTER

- How are you playful?
- How do you cultivate a natural love for learning?
- How do you practice playful pedagogy—trying new things in your practice?

Inquiry Teachers Teach Slowly
NOVICE ← 1 2 3 4 5 → MASTER

- How do you teach slowly?
- Are you more concerned with helping your students become master learners or more concerned with covering content?
- How do you let learning unfold and blossom at a pace empowering your learners?

Inquiry Teachers Know Their Curriculum
NOVICE ← 1 2 3 4 5 → MASTER

- How well do you know your curriculum?

- How can you cultivate a deeper understanding of what you'd like your learners to understand?
- How do you creatively connect learner passions, interests, and wonderings to your curriculum?
- How do you feel a sense of freedom when you reflect on your curriculum?

Inquiry Teachers Know Their Students
NOVICE ← 1 2 3 4 5 → MASTER

- How well do you know your students?
- How well do you know their stories, passions, interests, and curiosities?
- How well do you know their learning needs and empower them to understand these as well?
- How do you actively plan building relationship and trust in your classroom?

Inquiry Teachers Reflect and Revise as They Go
NOVICE ← 1 2 3 4 5 → MASTER

- How do you reflect and revise as you go?
- How do you tinker with your practice both *during* learning and *outside* of learning?
- How do your wonderings and observations guide your practice and inform your decisions?

Inquiry Teachers Go outside to Come Back inside
NOVICE ← 1 2 3 4 5 → MASTER

- How do you "go outside" to come back inside?
- How are you a connected educator?
- Who makes up your PLN of critical friends who challenge your understanding and support your growth?

Inquiry Teachers Are Curious
NOVICE ← 1 2 3 4 5 → MASTER

- How are you a curious teacher?
- How do you share your curiosities and wonderings?
- How do you actively model your questions for your learners through role play, provocations, and your own curiosities?

Inquiry Teachers Are Passionate
NOVICE ← 1 2 3 4 5 → MASTER

- How are you a passionate educator?
- How do you demonstrate your love for the classroom and learning with your students?
- How are you a lifelong learner?
- How do you find joy in your role as a teacher?

Keep this Inquiry Teacher: Elevate Your Mindset reflection in mind as you read *Inquiry Mindset*. Make note of the big ideas, the supportive structures, and the richly authentic resources and examples we include, and consider ways to use them to improve in areas where you need to grow and enhance the areas in which you're already strong. Inquiry learning can be messy—for teachers and for students! So when things feel uncertain or even scary, we want to encourage you to remain steadfast in your commitment to become the teacher your students need. Let this essential question guide you throughout your reading: *How will you enter the classroom after having completed your reading of* Inquiry Mindset *a different and more complete teacher than ever before?*

With every question you ask and with every discovery you make, you sharpen your own inquiry mindset.

How will you enter the classroom after having completed your reading of *Inquiry Mindset* a different and more complete teacher than ever before?

#INQUIRYMINDSET IN ACTION

After completing the Inquiry Teacher: Elevate Your Mindset reflection, share to our *#InquiryMindset* community a few of the strengths you identified possessing as an inquiry teacher. Where did you reflect the strongest traits and understandings using the Inquiry Teacher: Elevate Your Mindset reflection? Include one resource, activity, tool, or detail to help support our *#InquiryMindset* community members to elevate **their own mindset**. For example, if you scored highly in *Inquiry Teachers Know Their Students* category, what resource, activity, tool or detail can you share to help other readers grow in this area?

10 REASONS TO USE INQUIRY-BASED LEARNING

After I (Trevor) wrote *Dive into Inquiry*, my friend and colleague Sylvia Duckworth and I collaborated on a sketchnote entitled "10 Reasons to Use Inquiry-Based Learning." When we began the project, we wanted to inform and inspire educators about why inquiry is such powerful pedagogy. We also hoped to encourage teachers to reflect on their own practice and consider how they could make changes to truly amplify learning and empower student voice. The response to our sketchnote has been fantastic; amazing things happen when images, symbols, and art are applied to ideas and concepts.

Rebecca and I have used this sketchnote countless times while working to help educators integrate inquiry into their practice. It is a great starting point for learning as we challenge teachers to reflect on their own practices and consider their own classrooms. During

workshops and training sessions, we always ask, "Which of these ten reasons would we witness if we visited your school and watched you teach?"

Now, we'd like to ask you the same question. Take a look at the sketchnote and consider on how (or whether) your teaching reflects ten reasons for or benefits of inquiry. Are there some you do better than others? Are there any requiring more of your focus, support, and attention? Be specific as you describe what you do to foster these benefits in your practice, nurture them, and make them part of your learning culture.

 Do your learners feel like anything is possible when they come to class? They should.

NURTURE STUDENT PASSIONS AND TALENTS

You know the passions and talents your students possess and weave them into your classroom. You can speak about each learner and describe what each loves to do. You know your curriculum; you know your teaching area. You feel comfortable helping your learners demonstrate their understanding of the curriculum by sharing what they love. You nurture these passions and talents by helping your students explore them more deeply in your time together.

EMPOWER STUDENT VOICE AND HONOUR STUDENT CHOICE

You help your students understand their learning needs and put ~~~~~~~~ onouring their voic and direction in y nities in multi- ple red, confident, and flexibility and opti

[Handwritten note overlaid on page:]

10 Reasons to use inquiry - based learning

1) nurture Student passions / talents

2) empower Student voce and honour student choice

3) increase motivation and engagement

4) Foster curiosity and a love for learning

5) teach grit, perseverance, growth mindset, self-regulation

S om, and they enjoy re genuinely engag ant and tran-scend new things, are energized in your classroom, and, for the most part, are on task.

FOSTER CURIOSITY AND A LOVE FOR LEARNING

Your students' curiosities and interests have a place in your classroom and are explored in a meaningful way. You demonstrate that learning doesn't always begin with you; their curiosities can lead too. You help your students make connections between their curiosities and interests and your curriculum and your assessment of their learning.

workshops and training sessions, we always ask, "Which of these ten reasons would we witness if we visited your school and watched you teach?"

Now, we'd like to ask you the same question. Take a look at the sketchnote and consider on how (or whether) your teaching reflects ten reasons for or benefits of inquiry. Are there some you do better than others? Are there any requiring more of your focus, support, and attention? Be specific as you describe what you do to foster these benefits in your practice, nurture them, and make them part of your learning culture.

Do your learners feel like anything is possible when they come to class? They should.

NURTURE STUDENT PASSIONS AND TALENTS

You know the passions and talents your students possess and weave them into your classroom. You can speak about each learner and describe what each loves to do. You know your curriculum; you know your teaching area. You feel comfortable helping your learners demonstrate their understanding of the curriculum by sharing what they love. You nurture these passions and talents by helping your students explore them more deeply in your time together.

EMPOWER STUDENT VOICE AND HONOUR STUDENT CHOICE

You help your students understand their learning needs and put words to them. You empower your students by honouring their voice. Your students help shape the learning culture and direction in your classroom, and you provide learning opportunities in multiple ways and at multiple times. Students feel empowered, confident, and capable of success because they know you provide flexibility and options to support their learning needs.

INCREASE MOTIVATION AND ENGAGEMENT

Students look forward to coming to your classroom, and they enjoy your class. They are motivated to learn and are genuinely engaged in class. They believe that the learning is relevant and transcends your time with your students. Students try new things, are energized in your classroom, and, for the most part, are on task.

FOSTER CURIOSITY AND A LOVE FOR LEARNING

Your students' curiosities and interests have a place in your classroom and are explored in a meaningful way. You demonstrate that learning doesn't always begin with you; their curiosities can lead too. You help your students make connections between their curiosities and interests and your curriculum and your assessment of their learning.

TEACH GRIT, PERSEVERANCE, GROWTH MINDSET, AND SELF-REGULATION

Your students don't get down on themselves when they miss their goals. They see these moments in learning as *opportunities to be better*, not as shortcomings or failures. They know how to reflect and revise to achieve growth. Your students roll with the punches; they may get down but they *always* bounce back.

MAKE RESEARCH MEANINGFUL AND DEVELOP STRONG RESEARCH SKILLS

Your students are research savvy; they know how to locate rich, relevant, and accurate information. They know the difference between searching Wikipedia, Google, and, for older students, an academic database such as EBSCO. They know how to locate resources in your classroom and your school's library. You make the research process meaningful by explicitly connecting *what* students are researching to *why* they are researching it. Your students are digitally literate.

DEEPEN UNDERSTANDING TO GO BEYOND MEMORIZING FACTS AND CONTENT

You focus on big ideas in your classroom, and they guide your instruction and shape learning opportunities for your students. Conceptual understandings drive your units of study and content, and facts come alive and hold relevance for your students because you tie them to these big ideas. Your students can communicate the big ideas.

If students dump the contents of their binders in the trash at the end of the school year, we haven't done our jobs. Relevant learning doesn't get tossed.

FORTIFY THE IMPORTANCE OF ASKING GOOD QUESTIONS

Questions play an important role in your classroom. You give learners the time and support to grapple with and explore questions using a variety of sources and means. Learning begins with a question, whether it's yours or your students'. Your students know the difference between closed and open questions, and you discuss both in your classroom.

ENABLE STUDENTS TO TAKE OWNERSHIP OVER THEIR OWN LEARNING AND TO REACH THEIR GOALS

You share ownership of learning *with* your students. Your learners freely share ideas and, at times, even lead or teach their peers. Students set goals, strive to attain them, and reflect on and revise their learning pathway to help them hit their target.

SOLVE THE PROBLEMS OF TOMORROW IN THE CLASSROOMS OF TODAY

Students learn the twenty-first century skills needed to become the problem solvers, critical thinkers, and inspired innovators our world needs. Communication, collaboration, creativity, and critical thinking are discussed, used, and nurtured in your classroom. Students see learning in your room as ideas, problems, and challenges demanding their voices and their expertise.

You've now identified current evidence of inquiry in your classroom and likely pinpointed a few areas that require growth. This knowledge will make *Inquiry Mindset* all the more personal to you as you consider how to achieve the inquiry classroom you desire to create. Combined with your reflection from the previous chapter, you've created a blueprint for your professional growth in adopting inquiry as your own. Keep this blueprint in mind during your reading, and revisit your reflections as you read and as you return to your practice to make mindful changes and additions to your craft.

#INQUIRYMINDSET IN ACTION

Upon reflecting on the *10 Reasons to Use Inquiry-based Learning* sketchnote, share a few of the reasons that currently exist in your teaching and how you foster these each and every day in your classroom. For example, if you identified **fortify the importance of asking good questions** as an existing characteristic in your classroom, what do you do to actively ensure this occurs?

Along with our previous *#InquiryMindset in Action* from chapter 1, our readers will now have access to a diverse range of powerful resources, activities and ideas that they can use to accelerate their adoption of inquiry in their practice. Have a look at what others have shared and reflect on how you can use these resources to accelerate your own growth throughout your reading. Remember, in inquiry we are all better together!

THE INQUIRY CYCLE

Sharing the learning process with our students—gradually releasing control over learning from the teacher to the student—and having students follow their passions, curiosities, and wonderings are unique benefits afforded by the inquiry model. Honing twenty-first-century skills and facilitating authentic learning are powerful reasons to adopt inquiry as your own. But from the outside looking in, the inquiry classroom can appear overwhelming, untraditional, and, at times, even messy. The idea of having an entire classroom of young learners engaged in inquiry can be daunting for those unaccustomed to the structures and processes the inquiry teacher uses.

In this chapter, we provide some clear and accessible steps to help you map out your unique inquiry journey. You can help your learners by mindfully preparing and planning your inquiry approach. The process we practice in our classrooms helps you make the most of adopting inquiry as your own. Whether you're in the structured end of the inquiry pool, planning all these phases in their entirety, or you're in the free inquiry end of the pool, in which your students are creating their own essential questions and have more agency in their research, the inquiry phases outlined here will support you to be successful.

> Sharing the learning process with our students—gradually releasing control over learning from the teacher to the student— and having students follow their passions, curiosities, and wonderings are unique benefits afforded by the inquiry model.

To help make your inquiry successful, when planning your own inquiry unit of study, keep three specific things in mind: your learners, your curriculum, and your assessment.

KEEP YOUR LEARNERS IN MIND

As stated previously, inquiry teachers know their students. Understanding the needs, stories, and wonderings of their students allows the inquiry teacher to powerfully plan learning experiences and units of study. Reflect on the skills and understandings your learners have honed throughout your school year and how these can support the inquiry you are embarking on. Consider their interests and curiosities and how these could be explored more meaningfully in connection to your curriculum. And think about what challenges may surface for each of your learners in the inquiry you are planning. This reflection concerning your students will help you better meet their unique learning needs.

KEEP YOUR CURRICULUM IN MIND

Reflect on what curricular objectives you want students to explore in your inquiry. Identify precisely what you hope your students will *learn* throughout this unit of study. Pinpoint what artifacts, provocations, learning experiences, and resources you will weave into the inquiry to support your students' learning. And think about how this unit of study supports the growth and collective learning you have mapped out for your students for the entire school year.

KEEP YOUR ASSESSMENT IN MIND

Finally, identify how you will assess understanding throughout learning (formative) and at the conclusion of the inquiry unit (summative). These decisions can be based on skills and competencies your learners need to know and demonstrate or on learning objectives you haven't yet assessed. Additionally, these decisions can be based on how your learners *want* to demonstrate their understanding. By empowering students to choose how they would like to show their learning, we enable them to tap into their strengths, interests, and learning styles. When students have agency over assessment, the teacher benefits greatly by obtaining a clearer understanding of what the student learned. Gone are the anxieties and concerns surfacing during assessment; in their place, grows confidence, clarity, and engagement.

 When students choose how they would like to show their learning, they to tap into their strengths, interests, and learning styles. Amazing things happen.

10 PHASES OF THE INQUIRY CYCLE

1. Determine Your Focus
2. Start with an Essential Question
3. Brainstorm Questions
4. Brainstorm Subtopics
5. Select a Subtopic
6. Access Prior Knowledge
7. Identify Wonderings
8. Research
9. Make Cross-Curricular Connections
10. Perform, Reflect, and Revise

We have broken down each phase and included a case study example to illustrate what this could look like in your classroom.

Phase 1: Determine Your Focus

Consider the Four Pillars of Inquiry, which are explained in more detail in Chapter 6. The Four Pillars represent powerful entry points into inquiry. Determine which pillar—Explore a Passion, Aim for a Goal, Delve into Your Curiosities, and Take on a New Challenge—will guide your inquiry focus. Perhaps your inquiry will be tied to curiosities, a goal or an outcome, a passion, or a challenge.

Determining this first is critical as you look at the entire unit of study and plan the artifacts, provocations, learning experiences, and resources you will weave into the classroom experience. Consider using a provocation to stir questions, ignite curiosities, and shape your inquiry. Provocations are images, videos, or artifacts that are used to engage learners in inquiry. Provocations are discussed in more detail in Chapter 11.

Case Study Example: *Animals* (Your chosen topic can come from curiosities and a desired curricular outcome.)

Phase 2: Start with an Essential Question

Begin your inquiries, units, and lessons with an essential question. Depending on which type of inquiry you plan, this question could come from you or from your learners. Framing your unit of study in an essential question allows your students to participate in an entirely different learning experience—one in which they are genuinely engaged and able to explore a rich variety of resources and which, over time, gradually flips control of learning from the teacher to the learner.

Case Study Example: *How do animals survive?*

Phase 3: Brainstorm Questions

Brainstorming explores further questions connected to the essential question. By creating a list of sub-questions, you and your students will gain a clearer picture of where your inquiry will take you. These questions help formulate your research plans and what other artifacts and resources you will need to explore with your students.

We love this phase because it relies on students' curiosity and voice; they always come up with questions, ideas, and angles beyond our wildest imaginings. When necessary, we present sub-questions to our students to model the brainstorming process for them and ensure that our inquiry plan leads to the curricular objectives we aim to explore for a particular unit of study.

Case Study Example: What do animals eat? What do animals do in the different seasons? How do animals protect themselves? Which animals interest us?

Phase 4: Brainstorm Subtopics

After identifying questions with your students, shift your focus to subtopics. Ask students to identify patterns or trends emerging from the questions previously brainstormed. Then create headings for these identified subtopics.

Remind students that it's okay if our inquiry changes based on the interests and ideas arising from your class discussions and research. This phase is exciting! It's important that learners feel that they have a genuine impact on your inquiry plans. As they voice their interests and wonderings and you add these to your inquiry unit, your students will feel a sense of belonging, purpose, and direction—powerful additions to the classroom!

 Follow where inquiry takes you. Follow your curiosities. Follow new understandings. They will lead you to unexpectedly exciting new destinations.

Case Study Example: To encourage students to learn about animals and how they survive, provide them with four or five different animals on which to focus. From those animals, students can then choose the one they find most interesting. Each learner's goal is to discover how his or her chosen animal survives and adapts to the different seasons.

Phase 5: Select a Subtopic

Look at the brainstormed list of subtopics together and invite learners to choose the topic most interesting to them. Divide students into groups based on their choices.

We may suggest that students pick their top two choices to allow us flexibility to make our group sizes as even as possible while honouring the students' choices. Consistent group sizes support sharing research tools and books and enable strong collaborations.

Case Study Example: Five students pick bears, five pick coyotes, seven pick hummingbirds, and four pick salmon.

Phase 6: Access Prior Knowledge

Students work together in small groups to brainstorm as much information as they can about their chosen topic. We call this creating "What We Know" lists. Have them record their ideas and current understanding on the white board or in their inquiry journals. You can also ask students to share their brainstorms using a digital brainstorming tool such as Padlet. This will allow you to seamlessly add these rich artifacts of learning to their digital portfolios.

Case Study Example: Students may list things such as *"I know bears can . . . hibernate, catch salmon, and stay warm because of their thick fur."*

Phase 7: Identify Wonderings

Prompt learners to review their lists of facts and ideas and share any questions or wonderings they have. You may want to prompt younger learners by asking questions such as, *What is missing? What would you like to know more about? What do you wonder about the topic? If you could learn anything else about your topic, what would it be?* Most often students identify their own wonderings—what they will explore as their individual portion of the group's inquiry. Some groups may identify a wondering they want to explore together.

Case Study Example: *I wonder whether bears get hungry during hibernation. I wonder whether bears have a good sense of smell. Do bears stay together in packs like wolves?*

Phase 8: Research

Once your students have created their "What We Know" lists and shared their wonderings, it's time to begin the research phase of the inquiry journey. Typically, groups research different topics at the same time.

To support our learners in this personal inquiry experience, we equip students with tools and a process to help them stay organized.

We give our younger learners a research booklet where they record what they learn. The booklet, approximately eight half-pages, contains several prompts to drive their research, questioning, and learning. We propose that our youngest learners document their research through illustrations, using initial word sounds to label objects in their illustrations. Adding one or two words or full thoughts and wonderings scribed by an adult can be powerful.

We invite you to expand this based on the readiness and age of your learners. Instead of a half-page booklet, use larger research books or digital versions on Google Slides. Start with a title page, provide space for students to illustrate and write about their wondering, and include various prompts. Some of our favourite prompts are:

- Describe the appearance of [your topic] and label its parts
- What does [your topic] do?
- What changes occur for [your topic] because of environment?
- What needs does [your topic] have?
- What unique facts did you discover about [your topic]?

These prompts easily adapt to any inquiry topic and reflect the important characteristics—*need to know* information—of a specific inquiry.

Every student uses a research booklet no matter their topic. We tend to progress through the research together; students are always on the same page of their booklets whether we are using nonfiction resource books, Kiddle (a visual search engine for kids), child-friendly websites, or Research Mats (discussed in Chapter 8).

Earlier in this chapter, we encouraged you to reflect on your students, your curriculum, and your assessment and asked you to identify your learning goals and curricular objectives, your provocations and resources, and your formative and summative assessment tools. During the research phase, keep in mind this initial inquiry unit planning. Weave students' artifacts into the inquiry journey to ensure that they learn what you had planned. Reflect and revise throughout this phase to ensure that each student attains the understanding and skills you intend. Differentiate and scaffold where needed to best support learners who may require more time and care than others.

Case Study Example: Some prompts we use for our case study research booklet are about needs, appearance, habitat, and seasonal changes, and how all of these affect the animal's life.

Phase 9: Make Cross-Curricular Connections

Once the research phase is underway, consider introducing new provocations to see what further questions, wonderings, and curiosities might be sparked in your inquiry.

We actively seek opportunities to nurture connections to other topics we are learning about. These natural threads across topics transcend disciplines and subjects and help our learners understand the rich interconnectedness of all things in our world. Whether students are engaged in a science experiment discovered on Pinterest, a journal reflection about their learning in language arts, a nature walk and mapping activity for social studies, or a gym game mimicking bats' echolocation, a single topic related to animals can lead to many rich learning experiences.

Case Study Example: Take the research and observations from the groups and use the behaviour of their animals to create a fun and interactive game for gym class or physical activity. Challenge each group to design their own game and teach it to the class.

Phase 10: Perform, Reflect, and Revise

Sharing understanding is the final phase of the inquiry journey. Provide opportunities for your students to receive formative feedback throughout this process, and equip them with the language and understanding to self-assess their work. Build in time to reflect and revise both before their demonstrations of understanding and after feedback is given. Be mindful of these supportive structures and consider ways to empower students to grow and improve throughout the inquiry unit. Consider weaving in a public display of understanding during this phase to broaden the audience witnessing the students' amazing learning and the hard work and determination they demonstrated. We explain a few ways this can be done in Chapter 10.

> **Case Study Example:** Student groups create art murals to depict what their animals need to survive (habitat, food, protection, etc.). Consider providing bulletin board space for large murals or poster boards for small group murals.

Now that you have a clear process in mind that supports how inquiry can be planned in your classroom, it's time to explore the Types of Student Inquiry and begin to look more closely at inquiry throughout your practice.

#INQUIRYMINDSET IN ACTION

At the onset of this chapter, we asked you to **keep your learners in mind, keep your curriculum in mind,** and **keep your assessment in mind**. This advice will aid you in planning inquiry in your classroom. Reflect on lessons and units of learning you have done in the past or have planned for your students in the near future. Is there something that, with some slight tweaking or revision, would connect powerfully with the Inquiry Cycle? In reflecting on this chapter, we challenge you to make those tweaks and revisions, put your inquiry plan into action, and share this process with our *#InquiryMindset* community.

TYPES OF
STUDENT INQUIRY

When I (Trevor) first adopted an inquiry approach in my classroom, I discovered that when students explore a topic they are truly passionate about, amazing things happen: engagement increases, attendance and work ethic improve, twenty-first-century skills are acquired, classroom energy and collaboration are fostered, and my assessment of student understanding becomes more clear and accurate.

One early experience with a student in inquiry convinced me I was on to something. His name was Chris.

Chris was a shy, introverted student in my senior-level English class. Throughout the course I saw Chris raise his hand during a class discussion only once, and it was to ask permission to use the washroom. He didn't like sharing, and he certainly didn't come across as a confident student. But when it came time to explore a passion in the form of a free inquiry project, Chris showed me a side of him that I didn't know existed.

Chris was an avid reader of fantasy novels and a dedicated artist. For his free inquiry project, Chris researched the essential question *how can symbolism deepen the reader's understanding of theme in a fantasy novel series?* Chris decided to demonstrate his understanding in the form of a collection of paintings he would create and present in a gallery walk with our class. His plan for this presentation was thorough. He would complete twelve paintings for the four novels he explored. He would write an artist statement introducing his audience to the aim and scope of his collection. Each painting would be accompanied by a short written description of how Chris discovered symbolism in his reading and how symbolism was represented in each particular painting. He would then lead his classmates through a question-and-answer period to conclude the gallery walk.

When Chris's presentation day came, we were all amazed by his talents. First, Chris spoke confidently about his collection. He knew his stuff, and he clearly loved sharing his research. Chris spoke more during his presentation than he had during the entire rest of the course. Speaking about something he was genuinely interested in and passionate about made all the difference in Chris's confidence. Second, his artwork was enchanting. To say he was a "good artist" would be an understatement. Each painting was unique in its portrayal of symbolism, yet together the collection possessed powerful synergies from piece to piece. The class was enthralled with his presentation.

During the Q&A portion of the gallery walk, one student asked Chris how he had become such a strong artist. Chris's answer blew us all away. He shared that throughout his primary years in school, he didn't speak. From kindergarten through grades one and two, Chris didn't say a single word in school. Instead, he drew in his notebooks. He scribbled and sketched for three straight years rather than print or talk. Early in grade three, Chris underwent some testing with a school counsellor, and it was discovered that he was dyslexic. Chris's drawing was a coping mechanism in his world of uncertainty. Because he didn't understand what was happening in class, he tried to make sense of it through drawing. Now, years later, it was these early and frustrating years in school that formed the talent we were witnessing in class. Chris's honesty was an incredibly moving experience for us all.

It was stories like Chris's that convinced me that I needed to explore more opportunities to provide students with free inquiry projects in class. I was certain that this would yield similar powerful experiences for other learners. However, the very next year some of my students felt overwhelmed and underprepared for this personalized approach to learning. They were anxious in free inquiry, and on reflection, I felt I was to blame. I had forced them into the deep end of the inquiry pool without helping them acquire the necessary skills and understandings to be successful with this increased agency over learning. This is where the Types of Student Inquiry come into play.

The Types of Student Inquiry is a scaffolded approach to inquiry in the classroom, gradually increasing student agency over learning while providing learners with the necessary skills, knowledge, and understanding to be successful in their inquiry.

Introducing the Types of Student Inquiry early in the year is important. In the coming months, we break down how these will shape our learning and subsequent time. Inquiry is most successful when strongly scaffolded; therefore, we create an inquiry scope and sequence for the entire year. Simply put, we begin in a Structured Inquiry model, transition to a Controlled Inquiry, continue to a Guided Inquiry and, if all goes well, conclude with a Free Inquiry. Since these types reflect four large units of study, all framed by an essential question with elements of inquiry evident throughout, we organize our school year into these quarters and spend equal time in each type of inquiry.

Scaffolding is critical to our inquiry journey. Too often teachers enter the inquiry pool in the deep end, heading straight to Free Inquiry, as I had done with Chris. We can't blame them; the essential questions students ask and the demonstrations of learning students create are incredibly meaningful and resonate with their audience. But beginning your adoption of inquiry by diving right into Free Inquiry could result in overwhelmed and underprepared inquiry students. In our experience, without flipping control in the classroom, empowering student learning, and scaffolding with the Types of Student Inquiry, students will not feel as confident, supported, or empowered through our inquiry journey.

 Don't throw your learners into the deep end of the inquiry pool without empowering them with the Types of Student Inquiry first.

The Types of Student Inquiry help equip our students to feel confident in their inquiry journey. They ensure students are connected to their learning, certain of how to explore their passions, interests, and curiosities, and comfortable with their role. The Types of Student Inquiry continue the gradual release of control of our learning that we started at the beginning of the course.

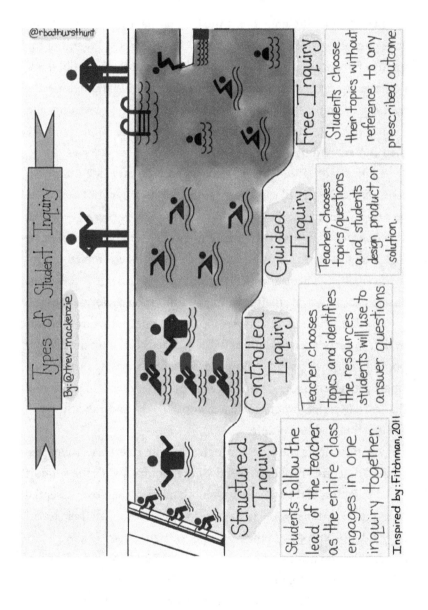

THE FOUR TYPES OF STUDENT INQUIRY

Structured: Students follow the lead of the teacher as the entire class engages in one inquiry together. On the Structured end of the inquiry pool, the teacher has complete control of the essential question, the resources students will use to create understanding, specific learning evidence students will use to document their learning, and the performance task students will complete as a demonstration of their understanding.

Controlled: The teacher chooses topics and identifies the resources students will use to answer the questions. In the Controlled section of the inquiry pool, the teacher provides several essential questions for students to unpack. Students deepen their understanding through several resources the teacher has predetermined to provide valuable context and rich meaning to the essential questions. Students demonstrate their learning by a common performance task.

Guided: The teacher chooses topics and questions, and students design the product or solution. In the Guided section of the inquiry pool, the teacher further empowers student agency by providing a single (or selection of) essential questions for students to study, and the learner selects where to search for answers and how they will demonstrate understanding.

Free: Students choose their topics without reference to any prescribed outcome. In the deep end—Free inquiry—with the support and facilitation of the teacher, students construct their own essential question, research a wide array of resources, customize their learning evidence, and design their own performance task.

A common misconception of inquiry is that elementary learners will not be successful in Free Inquiry. We understand our colleagues' hesitancy to tackle thirty students working on thirty different essential questions. In this scenario, students are potentially seeking information from different resources and planning to demonstrate their learning in a unique fashion. We're often asked, "How can they be successful with this much independence?"

By the time we get to the Free Inquiry unit, we have spent considerable time unpacking inquiry, deepening our understanding of essential questions, and cultivating an inquiry mindset. We reflect on the design of each unit of learning and each Type of Student Inquiry. In doing so, we slowly add the powerful skills needed to be successful in Free Inquiry:

- Students have experienced a wide range of resources in a variety of formats.
- They have used a variety of tools to capture their learning (what we call Learning Evidence).
- And they have demonstrated their learning in a number of ways.

By the time we enter the Free Inquiry end of the inquiry pool, learners are more accustomed to their role as *inquirers*. They can identify their learning needs and how to harness the potential of inquiry in the classroom. The inquiry mindset they acquire helps curb the perceived risks of Free Inquiry in the younger grades. Additionally, the design of the course, by way of the Types of Student Inquiry, is scaffolded to support this final unit of Free Inquiry.

We love the Types of Student Inquiry framework because it provides us with a number of advantages to best prepare our learners for success in the inquiry classroom while simultaneously fostering a learning community to deepen understanding and nurture student agency. Some of these advantages are discussed in the following sections.

THE "MUST-KNOW" CONTENT COMES BEFORE FREE INQUIRY

As educators, one of the pillars of mastering our craft is knowing our curriculum and knowing it well, and a certain amount of "must-know" content exists in our classrooms. A deep understanding of these prescribed (and often standardized) learning objectives allows us to weave these into everything we do throughout the year. But striking a balance between these outcomes and the inquiry mindset is a challenge every inquiry teacher faces. The Types of Student Inquiry provide us with the structure to ensure that this balance is achieved. We frontload the must-know content into the Structured, Controlled, and, at times, the Guided units, enabling us to gather evidence that our students have created a deep understanding of our classroom's learning objectives by the time we get to Free Inquiry. Even so, the Free Inquiry unit doesn't abandon these important outcomes; on the contrary, we ensure that all learning in the Free Inquiry side of the inquiry pool meets the learning standards of our classroom. By scaffolding, using the Types of Student Inquiry, students are empowered to reflect on their learning and even identify these learning objectives *on their own*. This agency is a gift afforded by the gradual release of control over learning that frames our inquiry classroom.

 A gradual release of control over learning from the teacher to the learner allows educators to better meet the needs of today's student.

USING THE TENETS OF
UNDERSTANDING BY DESIGN

Understanding by Design (UbD) is the design framework we use to map our learning throughout the year. Also referred to as *backwards design*, UbD is the most powerful and supportive framework we've found to plan units of study. Authored by Jay McTighe and Grant Wiggins, UbD is a planning process and structure guide to curriculum, assessment, and instruction. If you've tinkered with inquiry, you've likely adopted the UbD framework into your practice.

UbD's two key ideas are found in its title: focus on teaching and assessing for understanding and learning transfer, and design the curriculum "backward" from those ends.

We love UbD for several reasons. First, it calls for educators to plan with the end in mind by first clarifying the learning they seek and identifying the desired learning results they aim to achieve. Second, UbD asks educators to think about the assessment evidence needed to show that students have achieved the desired learning. Finally, UbD teachers plan the means to the end, the teaching, the learning activities, and the resources to scaffold understanding and help students achieve the goals.

We also love UbD because it makes sense. If the performance task for our students is to use a variety of comprehension strategies to deepen learning during reading, UbD calls for us to plan our unit from this end. To use these strategies, students need to accomplish many smaller yet pivotal tasks leading up to this performance task. If we work backward from the performance task, we support our students through scaffolding the following skills and strategies:

- summarizing
- sequencing
- inferencing

- comparing and contrasting
- drawing conclusions
- self-questioning
- accessing prior knowledge

All of these examples would provide the knowledge base, skills, and preparation necessary to execute the performance task and use a variety of comprehension strategies to deepen learning during reading.

In the middle school and high school inquiry classroom, we explicitly discuss the tenets of UbD with our students. This strengthens their ability to successfully plan, initiate, revise, and execute a Free Inquiry unit of their own. Furthermore, learners who better grasp UbD become adept at improving their performance task. This is especially powerful with our younger learners. Through demonstrating how a performance task is scaffolded through formative assessments, rich and meaningful feedback, and building of skills, we have witnessed students tune in to what they can do to improve their work and enrich their understanding. Together we cultivate a metacognitive foundation to learning—a pivotal step toward nurturing an inquiry mindset.

> A metacognitive foundation to learning is a pivotal step toward nurturing an inquiry mindset.

The UbD framework can be applied to any future unit planning or goal setting students will face. It equips learners to identify their target, plan their steps toward attaining this goal, and take action toward achieving the goal. In each Type of Student Inquiry, we outline the unit from end to beginning, using a common language to help deepen student understanding of UbD. The impact of this planning structure on the inquiry mindset is powerful!

The Types of Student Inquiry graphic is posted in our classroom, and we refer to it often throughout our learning. As we transition from Structured to Controlled to Guided, we constantly reflect on more than the essential question and resources we are interacting with. We discuss our learning, our collaboration with one another, and the scaffolding of our learning toward a performance task. The marrying of inquiry and the tenets of *Understanding by Design* allow these rich learning opportunities to occur.

TWENTY-FIRST-CENTURY LEARNERS, AKA THE INQUIRY MINDSET

The Types of Student Inquiry allow us to touch on many of the soft skills necessary to navigate today's world, a world in which certain hallmarks of the traditional classroom—memorization of facts and performance of routine tasks—are becoming less important. Curiosity, creativity, initiative, multidisciplinary thinking, and empathy prepare learners for a constantly changing world. Add in growth mindset, grit, and character, and we more clearly see how inquiry-based learning and the Types of Student Inquiry provide a structure to best prepare students for future challenges.

Following are a few inquiry "cards" and the main components of each unit. These break down the Types of Student Inquiry as they would unfold in a variety of grade levels and subjects. Feel free to use these as the beginnings of inquiry in your own classroom.

The classroom of yesterday relied on the memorization of facts and the performance of routine tasks, and this isn't good enough any longer. The classroom of tomorrow needs something different. The classroom of tomorrow needs the Types of Student Inquiry.

Type of Student Inquiry: Structured

Level and Subject: Primary Math

Essential Question: How can numbers be represented in different ways?

Resources, Artifacts, and Experiences: *Remarkable Cuisenaire Rods: Mathematical Tasks for Primary Classrooms* by Carole Fullerton, multiple sets of Cuisenaire rods, exploration time, printed and laminated numerals with associated dots.

Learning Evidence: In partners or individually, students will work toward matching Cuisenaire rods to numeral cards to demonstrate that each rod represents a numeral, and numbers and amounts can be represented by Cuisenaire rods.

Performance Task: Students will . . .

- explore with Cuisenaire rods
- work on ordering Cuisenaire rods from smallest to biggest to discover a size connection to numbers
- look for patterns and connections with numeral cards

Level and Subject: Primary Social Studies

Essential Question: How is First Peoples' history shared through stories?

Resources, Artifacts, and Experiences: An Elder, an Indigenous person of a certain age that has the honour of sharing about his or her culture, visits to share a cultural story and answer students' questions. Before the visit, brainstorm a list of questions to ask about the importance and history of storytelling in First Peoples' culture.

Learning Evidence: Students will use whiteboards to note answers to their questions throughout the Elder's visit. After the visit, students will participate in a whole-group sharing circle to reflect and share about their feelings, further questions, takeaways, and learning from the visit.

Performance Task: Students will . . .

- share a story important to them
- illustrate their story and write an accompanying piece sharing it

Level and Subject: Intermediate Science

Essential Question: What are Newton's three laws of motion?

Resources, Artifacts, and Experiences: Nonfiction books and Kiddle for online research

Learning Evidence: Students will be assigned to work in one of three focus groups. Each group will learn about one of Newton's laws of motion. Students will use a graphic organizer to document their understanding of the law of motion they are researching.

Performance Task: Each group will . . .

- work together to create a song, in any genre, explaining the law of motion

- share their song, providing the class with three short songs teaching Newton's three laws of motion

Type of Student Inquiry: Controlled

Level and Subject: Primary Science

Essential Question: What are the needs of the bears found in British Columbia?

Resources, Artifacts, and Experiences:
- nonfiction texts (hard copies)—Online *Reading A to Z* digital readers
- small world play provocation table, think about: bears, string, rocks, sticks, baskets as caves, natural blocks, play trees, etc.
- create a dramatic play cave area
- take part in a salmon egg tank school release program.
- read and retell Indigenous and local place-based stories about local animals
- complete an Indigenous or local artist study that ties into animal art

Learning Evidence: Through nonfiction research, students will complete a research guide template with prompts about appearance, habitat, food, seasonal changes, and interesting facts.

Performance Task: Students will . . .
- illustrate their animal
- use an iPad to take a photograph of their animal art
- choose one or two interesting facts to write out and rehearse
- use ChatterPix Kids (a free iPad app that you and your students can use to turn pictures into talking pictures) to

photograph their animal art and record an audio recording of their facts. These Chatterpix Kids projects will be shared out with the whole group and shared via their digital portfolios or student blogs.

Level and Subject: Primary Visual Arts

Essential Question: What kind of visual elements (line, shape, texture, colour, form, etc.) does Ted Harrison (a prominent local Canadian artist) use in his paintings?

Resources, Artifacts, and Experiences: A variety of examples of Ted Harrison's work and children's books: *Children of the Yukon*, *A Northern Alphabet*, and *O Canada*.

Learning Evidence: Graphic organizer to take brief notes and illustrate quick examples on the types of line, shape, texture, colours, or form used

Performance Task: Students will . . .
- choose one of Ted Harrison's pieces to recreate, using the provided materials in class
- reflect either orally or in writing about why they chose this piece and how they aim to represent Ted Harrison's art style through their own piece

Level and Subject: Intermediate Physical and Health Education

Essential Question: What are some connections between eating, physical activity, and mental wellbeing?

Resources, Artifacts, and Experiences: Nutritionist visits to explain the relationship between healthy eating and mental wellbeing. Students experience various types of physical activity (running, circuit training, team sports, yoga, dance, rock climbing, etc.) throughout the year in physical education.

Learning Evidence: Students will create questions for the nutritionist visit and take notes to track the answers to their questions. Students will also reflect on how they felt before, during, and after each physical activity block they participate in and record their reflections in their activity journals.

Performance Task: Students will . . .

- create a one-page advertisement highlighting the impacts that eating a balanced diet and being physically active have on our mental wellbeing. Students can illustrate the advertisement by hand or use Canva to create it digitally. It should be done with a student audience in mind and then shared with the class.
- create a slogan to go with their advertisement

Type of Student Inquiry: Guided

Level and Subject: Primary Science

Essential Question: How can objects move? Do objects move on their own? Must there be a force to move certain objects?

Resources, Artifacts, and Experiences: Fans and hairdryers for wind experiments in class, kite flying experiences outdoors, kite books, kite YouTube clips, trip to a kite-flying area, recycled materials, and art supplies and lots of tape!

Learning Evidence: Students will explore and research how objects move through exploration with wind and air. Students will record findings of what moves in the wind and what does not on a research chart template. Students will research kites and begin to discover what types of materials and design prototypes move best in the wind.

Performance Task: Students will . . .

- choose a kite shape they want to design and create a paper prototype
- explore outdoors or with fans and hair dryers to see how their prototype flies and moves in the wind. Based on their findings, they can reflect and revise their plans.
- choose materials to accompany their designs and create their kites
- travel to local kite-flying location to fly and experiment with their kites
- reflect orally on how their kites flew and what changes they would make next time

Level and Subject: Primary Mathematics

Essential Question: What are different ways to earn money to reach a financial goal?

Resources, Artifacts, and Experiences: As a class, read *Isabel's Carwash* by Sheila Blair.

Learning Evidence: As a whole group, brainstorm ways one might earn money to reach a financial goal (bake sale, household chores, helping neighbours with yard work, dog walking, popcorn sale, etc.). Come up with different options students find interesting and talk through the logistics of each idea.

Performance Task: Students will . . .

- choose one way to earn money that they wish to try. Students may work independently or in groups.
- must create a plan to support earning money in their chosen way
- have two weeks to carry out their earning plan. They must document, using either a journal entry each time they earn

money or using photographs to capture the stages of a bake sale–type project.

- share how their earning plan worked out and how much they earned at the end of the two weeks

The performance task could continue with students planning what to do with their money.

Level and subject: Intermediate Visual Arts

Essential Question: In what ways do artists communicate messages through their art?

Resources, Artifacts, and Experiences: YouTube exploration, local artists visiting as experts, local art experiences (art gallery trip, performance shows, etc.). Research about artists through nonfiction books, online searches, and reading of artists' blogs.

Learning Evidence: Students will experience various forms of art and look for ways artists communicate by using their art form. Students will have range and choice of how they research this: books, online, personal interviews, reading of blogs and articles, etc.

Performance Task: Students will . . .

- pick one artist or piece to examine
- share and reflect on what message they think the artist is trying to convey and how they think the artist does this. Students can consider questions such as "Do you think the artist meant to convey this message?" and "What other messages might audiences perceive from this art?"
- reflect through audio recording, still images of the art piece, an essay, or an oral presentation

If you feel you're ready to begin planning an inquiry unit, we suggest you start with a Structured Inquiry unit based on a topic you've taught before. We also recommend starting small and with the end in mind.

START WITH A STRUCTURED INQUIRY UNIT

When first adopting inquiry, it's easier to focus on a single essential question, resource, learning evidence, and performance task. We have found that starting with a Structured Inquiry unit allows our students to feel more confident in this new learning model. Furthermore, we are able to reflect on the design of the unit, the process of learning, and the role of the student in inquiry. Collectively, these build a strong foundation for our inquiry journey throughout the year. Start easy. Reflect. Try it again.

START WITH A TOPIC OR UNIT YOU HAVE TAUGHT BEFORE

Use a lesson or unit you have taught before and you feel truly resonated with your learners to take the dip into the inquiry pool. Reframe the lesson to begin with a powerful essential question. Because you are familiar and comfortable with the material, you'll be more comfortable with the reframing of how you get to the performance task.

START SMALL

You do not need to start with redesigning your whole year— or even a unit of study. Start small. Start with the single change of beginning your lessons and unit plans with essential questions. This will lead to a future of powerful and deep inquiry roots. Model these questions first. Demonstrate how they can lead to deeper learning. Then teach students how to ask essential questions of their own and use their essential questions to guide activities, lessons, resources, and performance tasks.

START WITH THE END IN MIND

Before you begin the journey of learning together, show your learners the target they are aiming for. This way, as students unpack information and create understanding, they already have their eyes on how they will eventually need to demonstrate what they are learning. The tenets of *Understanding by Design* present the structure to achieve this clarity and support.

#INQUIRYMINDSET IN ACTION

As we all know, rarely do lesson plans unfold perfectly in the classroom. Despite our careful planning and execution, teachers are amazingly skilled at reflecting in the moment and changing on the go. We learn from our mistakes and we never teach the same lesson twice.

The same goes for our students. Educators know that powerful learning happens when students make mistakes, when they reflect on their errors, and when they search for ways to improve, grow, and return to the process of learning better than before.

Reflect on the Types of Student Inquiry graphic. In your experience in inquiry, where have things gone sideways? Where has the messiness occurred? And how could this graphic support you in making subtle changes to support your *#InquiryMindset*? Please share with our *#InquiryMindset* community.

FREE INQUIRY

Free Inquiry, the most powerful Type of Student Inquiry, is the culmination of our journey through the inquiry pool together. Students have an abundance of agency over learning, allowing them to follow their passions and pursue their interests. Through the scaffolding presented by the Types of Student Inquiry, students have acquired a variety of inquiry skills and understandings that will allow them to be successful in Free Inquiry. They understand and can ask an essential question as well as a variety of closed questions. They can locate valuable and valid resources and research to gain understanding. They document their learning, and reflect and revise as they go. As inquiry teachers, our focus now shifts to more completely supporting our learners in exploring their creativity, curiosity, and dreams.

We must always be mindful of how our learners are feeling in inquiry and whether they will be successful in their Free Inquiry experience. If learners haven't acquired the skills to strengthen their inquiry and, perhaps more importantly, if they feel overwhelmed, anxious, or uncertain moving forward, we must shift our focus to differentiate to support them. If students are not ready for Free Inquiry, we scaffold accordingly. The inquiry classroom affords powerful opportunities to differentiate learning, especially in Free Inquiry. If our class did not succeed as we had hoped they would in Guided Inquiry, we spend more time honing the inquiry skills to better prepare them for Free Inquiry. However, if we are ready to enter the Free Inquiry end of the pool, we apply the framework, working models, and specific components we have developed and included in this chapter. Consider your learners before you roll out Free Inquiry to help you maximize the potential of following the passions, interests, and curiosities of your students.

Our learners love the Inquiry Process sketchnote because it suggests that a learning adventure awaits. Although bumps and challenges arise along the way, we can all use the map as a visual guide highlighting the various steps along our inquiry journey. We hang a large poster of this sketchnote in our class and refer to it often throughout the year. Learners can identify and share where we are in learning and where we are headed. This image paired with the Types of Student Inquiry graphic gives learners a firm grasp on the framework we'll operate under in inquiry. These contribute to students' success in their Free Inquiry unit, helping them stay on track and reflect and revise as they go, and creating a common structure we can all work under despite the high level of personalization we will achieve. We love how the Inquiry Process sketchnote ties together the tenets of UbD by showing a visual destination of our learning and the various steps we'll take in reaching it.

True personalized learning is only powerful after you've gotten to know your learners. Start there: Know your learners.

Dive into Inquiry proposes a plan and pitch framework to ensure that a successful inquiry unit is planned and executed. Students are asked to speak to a few key elements of their Free Inquiry unit so the teacher can ensure that their undertaking results in a successful outcome.

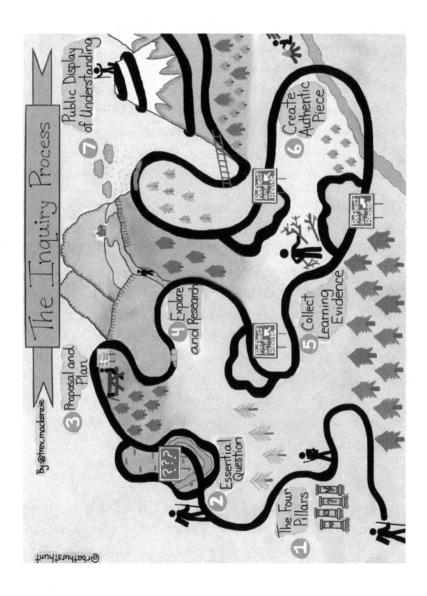

THE FREE INQUIRY PROPOSAL

1. What is your essential question? Please share why it is meaningful to you.
2. What is your authentic piece? How will you make your learning public?
3. What will you read, research, and study to help you explore your essential question?
4. What are your goals for your Free Inquiry?
5. What learning evidence will you gather to capture everything you are learning about your essential question?
6. What is your plan? Create a calendar and day-to-day plan to help your Free Inquiry unit be a successful learning experience.

We love seeing inquiry teachers of younger students apply this framework. When learners can speak or write to each point outlined in the plan and pitch, we know they have a firm grasp on the demands of their Free Inquiry unit. We don't suggest your students pitch you their unit of study for your approval. Nor do we believe their plan will have the same detail or ambition evident in the Free Inquiry proposals of our middle and high school learners. Rather, these points are most powerfully used when our younger learners can identify them, speak or write to them, and reflect on and personalize their journey to suit their interests and needs. Let's recap this process from *Dive into Inquiry* and break down the points to illustrate what they look like with our younger learners.

Section 1: What is your essential question? Please share why it is meaningful to you.

Learners share their essential question and why it is meaningful to them. Incredibly powerful things occur when students can describe why their learning is meaningful to them. In part, this

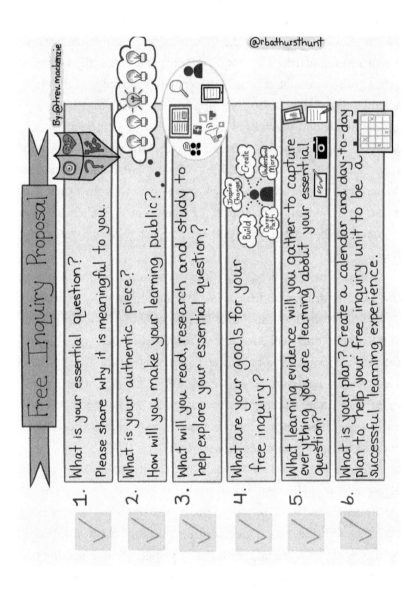

@rbathursthunt

By:@trev.mackenzie

Free Inquiry Proposal

1. What is your essential question? Please share why it is meaningful to you.

2. What is your authentic piece? How will you make your learning public?

3. What will you read, research and study to help explore your essential question?

4. What are your goals for your free inquiry?

5. What learning evidence will you gather to capture everything you are learning about your essential question?

6. What is your plan? Create a calendar and day-to-day plan to help your free inquiry unit to be a successful learning experience.

provides us with a clear understanding of *why* they've selected their inquiry topic and perhaps reveals some ways we can best support students in their inquiry endeavors. However, the most important reason we ask students why their learning is meaningful is because it illustrates *how* their learning is relevant and authentic. Learning outside of school should be no different from learning at school. By helping our students pursue learning relevant to them we are bridging the divide between school and life, a downfall of the over-standardized curricula we've witnessed in the traditional classroom. When students dig into something they are passionate about and share it with others, inevitably their engagement with their topic resonates with their audience and, at times, even inspires their peers.

Section 2: What is your authentic piece? How will you make your learning public?

Students identify how they'd like to demonstrate their learning and share it with an audience. We love holding a class, school, or community event (see the Public Display of Understanding chapter for ideas) and often ask our students to share their learning through a means we have agreed on as a learning community. To help them decide on an authentic piece, we ask them, "If you could demonstrate your understanding in any way, what would it be? Are you really good at something you feel would help communicate your understanding of your essential question?"

We love when students create a digital authentic piece for their demonstration of learning because it easily lives on, tends to engage the audience, and lends so well to public sharing of student learning via blogs, websites, social media, or any number of powerful apps, devices, and platforms making learning visible. We love helping our learners capture their understanding and share it with others!

Section 3: What will you read, research, and study to help explore your essential question?

Students identify what they will do, read, and watch to deepen understanding. Undoubtedly students capitalize on the expertise and support our teacher librarian provides (see the Explore and Research chapter for how this is done). They also make inherent connections between their plans for their Free Inquiry unit and research they've done before. Connecting to our experiences with our Wonder Wall, a visible curation of our wonderings in the classroom, and our living library of friends and family, the people we know that can support our research (both the Wonder Wall and the living library are explained in more detail in Chapter 7), students often chose to interview someone as part of their inquiry. We love these authentic and relevant strands in their Free Inquiry plans.

Section 4: What are your goals for your Free Inquiry?

Students identify a few goals for their Free Inquiry unit. It's so important for our younger learners to grasp that we do not learn for a grade or to receive a high mark in school. We encourage students to set highly personalized, meaningful, and achievable goals that impact them or those around them. Some students' goals from our past Free Inquiry units were . . .

- I want to engage and wow my audience.
- I want my learning to inspire my friends.
- I want my parents to be proud of my learning.
- I want to know something I didn't know before.

Students' goals inform the inquiry teacher how to best support learner inquiry and help them achieve their goals. As they work toward attaining them, amazing things happen!

> Students shouldn't 'learn for a grade' or 'to receive a high mark in school.' Empower students to set highly personalized, meaningful, and achievable goals—goals that make an impact on them or those around them.

Section 5: What learning evidence will you gather to capture everything you are learning about your essential question?

Students reflect on the learning evidence strategies and tools we have honed throughout the year and identify which they will use in their Free Inquiry unit. Whether they choose an inquiry folder, Flipgrid, Padlet, or even a Wonder Repository (some of these are outlined in Chapter 9, Making Inquiry Visible), our aim is for students to reflect and identify what works for their learning and to use this to support their Free Inquiry journey.

Section 6: What is your plan? Create a calendar and day-to-day plan to help your Free Inquiry unit be a successful learning experience.

Students map out the milestones of their Free Inquiry unit on a calendar template. Our middle school and high school learners complete a personal calendar that they reflect on and revise throughout their Free Inquiry unit to ensure success. However, we prefer that our younger learners do a collective calendar, one displayed in class, where we can pin our specific goals and plans. The inquiry teacher identifies particular due dates and check-in points, and students determine where their personalized due dates and check-ins will occur. Having this collaborative timeline publicly displayed allows the inquiry teacher to easily track and support our younger learners in the class. It also narrows our collective focus to the big ideas and milestones of the Free Inquiry unit. Throughout the unit, we will revisit this plan, and the inquiry teacher will help revise it where necessary. We all know it is rare for a plan to go from an idea to final execution perfectly, and the Free Inquiry unit is no different. Life can get in the way, and research can take us in unforeseen directions. The ability to revise throughout the inquiry process is an immensely valuable skill to ensure success.

We look for three elements in our learners' vision to ensure strong Free Inquiry units. Students' plans should be *achievable*, *grade level appropriate*, and *meaningful*.

FREE INQUIRY SHOULD BE ACHIEVABLE

Learners tend to dream big when they have agency over learning. The Free Inquiry unit is no different. The buildup to this highly exciting and inspiring time can lead learners to bite off more than they can chew. As we support students in planning their vision, we want to ensure that their inquiry is manageable and achievable. We look for whether students can successfully access, retrieve, and use the information they require in a timely and effective manner. We look for whether students can execute a performance task they will be proud of. Above all, we look at how we, the inquiry teacher, can best support them in their learning.

FREE INQUIRY MUST BE GRADE LEVEL APPROPRIATE

Free Inquiry is not *free time*. Although the agency over learning students experience can be powerfully freeing, there is always a connection between what they're learning and our curriculum. The learning objectives of our course are always visible and discussed throughout the year. Students need to be able to identify which learning objectives they've met and which ones they will focus on more intently in their Free Inquiry unit. Providing students with the language to understand and discuss these learning objectives is critical. We do this by making these targets visible in class, touching on them during learning experiences, and asking our learners to reflect and self-assess as we go. This ensures that Free Inquiry isn't just *free time*, and progress through learning is achieved by everyone involved.

> Free Inquiry is not *free time*. Although the agency over learning students experience can be powerfully freeing, there is always a connection between what they're learning and our curriculum.

FREE INQUIRY MUST BE MEANINGFUL TO THE LEARNER

As we noted in Section 1 of the proposal, Free Inquiry must be meaningful to the learner. When students can put into words how their inquiry is personally relevant, amazing things happen: Their learning connects to their world, their dedication to and engagement with their topic is heightened, and their audience is truly excited to hear more about their inquiry. They are much prouder of the end result than they would be with something prescribed or assigned by the teacher.

Now we shift our focus toward helping students identify their inquiry focus. In our classrooms, we use the opportunities afforded by the Four Pillars of Inquiry.

#INQUIRYMINDSET IN ACTION

Head to trevormackenzie.com and access the free high-resolution sketchnotes from *Inquiry Mindset*. In your classroom, show the *Inquiry Process* sketchnote to your students either on the projector screen or as a poster. Begin a class discussion by prompting your learners using these three powerful questions: **What do you notice? What do you know? What do you wonder?** As you'll be using this graphic more in your teaching in the coming months, introducing your students to the *Inquiry Process* sketchnote now and observing their answers and wonderings elicited from these prompts will provide you with many valuable insights into how to better meet their inquiry needs. As always, please share with our *#InquiryMindset* community.

THE FOUR PILLARS
OF INQUIRY

Inquiry-based learning can begin from many different inspirations, experiences, and passions. Defining an inquiry as you get started is important; we find it helpful to ground your learning, plan ahead, and reflect and revise as you go. The Four Pillars of Inquiry—*exploring a passion, aiming for a goal, delving into your curiosities,* and *taking on a new challenge*—provide the structure and support for you to empower your learners through this process. They also provide uniquely personalized foundations for inquiry experiences, allowing teachers and learners to set an inquiry focus, create a learning pathway, and identify a direction for research as they move forward. Each pillar is designed to provide an opportunity for learners to discover personal relevance in their classroom experience. Collectively, the pillars give all of our students an entry point into inquiry and agency over learning.

Exploring a passion allows a student or a group of students to embark on inquiry researching something they are passionate about.

Aiming for a goal guides students working toward achieving a specific goal or provides a framework for an inquiry teacher to meet a curriculum standard, learning target, or objective.

Delving into your curiosities occurs when inquiry begins from students' curiosities developed from a particular provocation, wondering, activity, or experience.

Taking on a new challenge is a great way to incorporate learning a new skill, creating, designing, or building into inquiry experiences.

These four pillars also support you, the inquiry teacher, to connect any inquiry to your curriculum. Let's look more closely at each pillar!

EXPLORE A PASSION

Exploring a passion is powerfully motivating for learners. Because passions come from the heart and reflect self-interest and intrigue, learners often possess a certain depth of prior knowledge about their passions. Most likely they have explored them before, grappled with the ups and downs of learning about them, and done personal reading or deeper research about them. Our youngest learners' passions tend to be things they know a lot about or things they are already involved in. These passions often create opportunities for deeper learning because students are highly motivated and willing to explore them further. Their prior knowledge of the topic accelerates and amplifies their inquiry.

Passions create opportunities for deeper learning as students are highly motivated and willing to explore them further. Their prior knowledge of the topic accelerates and amplifies their inquiry.

As we delve into exploring passions with our learners, we find it useful to give some examples to provide context, engagement, and motivation. We don't use examples or models to show learners explicitly *how* to do their inquiry; we aim to inspire our students through the positive impact of other young people.

QR Code
Caine's Arcade

Showing a video such as *Caine's Arcade*, as shared in *Dive into Inquiry*, provides learners with the opportunity to witness the impact a child can have when he follows his passion. It allows learners to visualize possibilities and prompts rich discussion and dissection of Caine's possible inquiry process. In our experience, this video fills learners with excitement and inspiration. We follow up the video with a whole-group discussion, asking numerous questions:

- What do you think Caine's passion is?
- How did he choose to share his passion?
- How do you think he might have done some research about his passion?
- What do you think Caine wondered about?
- What do you think he learned?
- Where do you think Caine might go next with his passion?

We then shift to learners sharing their own passions, following some of the proposed questions above. Dave Shortreed with the Greater Victoria School District describes his personal experience with using Caine's Arcade:

When I first came across the Caine's Arcade *video, I was immediately struck by how much ownership Caine had on his own projects and his learning. I shared the video to my grade five classes the very next day along with a pile of cardboard and other materials I had collected. My learners were excited and empowered by Caine's video. They immediately asked to begin.*

We framed an open question together: How can you make a game that someone else can play? What components would be needed to get someone really excited to play your game? They were challenged to make connections to our learning and to share their thinking out loud with our group. They began linking the project of building an arcade to our learning in math, science, and language arts. My learners were in the driver's seat the entire time. The enthusiasm from Caine's Arcade *drove this project from a Friday afternoon challenge to an inquiry project that spanned a few weeks. I worked with my learners by providing them with materials, time, and support. I stepped back and allowed my learners to embrace the energy that inquiry-based learning provided. It was a rich learning process to witness.*

What I noticed for my learners was how much their learning impacted one another. I saw students start and restart, without my input or initiative, and each time the projects were being tweaked and levelled up to improve in design, concept, and quality. I also noticed that although they were proud of their final projects, they enjoyed the process of making their game just as much as the outcome. I did a similar Caine's Arcade *activity in two different schools with two different demographics. In both schools, the outcome was very similar.*

Throughout these inquiry projects my learners were empowered and it showed through their excitement in the process as well as in their final products. Learning in the classroom was given a purpose, and the engagement level was high across the board because the task was accessible to everyone. This experience caused me to reflect on how I could create this kind of space again for my learners where they could take ownership of their own learning. I found that it was more about me letting go of the direction the learning could go as a teacher and simply begin learning by sharing an idea, a provocation, or a wondering and then supporting my learners in running with it. This type of learning flow did not have me pre-thinking each step, lesson, or curriculum connection because we co-created the learning and connections as we created.

AIM FOR A GOAL

Aiming for a goal can be an intensely rewarding, meaningful, and exciting experience for our learners. Students identify a personalized goal and set their sights on gaining deeper understanding as they work toward their objective. Older learners often aim for a goal geared toward a career path or a postsecondary journey. Aiming for a goal is most powerful with younger students when they work to learn or master a new skill.

Whether a student wishes to learn to dubstep, play the guitar, or knit, their motivation levels are high because they've identified an intrinsic goal. Setting up a framework and a timeline learners can follow to track their growth is one way to support this process. We love Josh Kaufman's twenty-hour timeline for learning a new skill, and we share part of it with our older learners. In a TED Talk, Josh shares how a new skill can be learned in twenty hours through deliberate and mindful practice. He clarifies the steps to learn a new skill:

"The First 20 Hours: How to Learn Anything" by Josh Kaufman

- Deconstruct the skill. *What do I hope to be able to do?*
- Look into the skill and break it down into smaller pieces or steps. *What are the smaller things I need to be able to do to acquire my overall skill?*
- Learn enough through resources, information, and research to be able to self-correct when practicing. *What mistakes did I make, and how can I self-correct to continue to improve?*
- Remove barriers and distractions. *How can I be most focused?*
- Commit to practice. *How can I set aside the time to begin practicing?*

This type of project can be powerful when younger learners buddy up with an older group, such as partnering kindergarten learners with a class of grade fives. Pairing your younger students with older buddies provides some amazing learning opportunities for everyone involved. As students get to know one another, they are prompted to find a common interest and goal. We encourage pairs to brainstorm skills they already possess, such as beading, painting, building, origami, knitting, and so forth. Second, the pairs brainstorm a list of skills they would like to learn and add these to their lists. Cooking, skateboarding, duct tape designing, sewing, and slam dunking are skills we've heard from past learners.

We continue to cycle back to Josh Kaufman's twenty-hour project and the steps outlined. Through this process, we support and empower students through a variety of types of research to learn more about the skills they hope to acquire. Some of our favourite vehicles for deepening understanding are:

- nonfiction books
- arts and crafts
- how-to experiment guidebooks
- YouTube tutorials
- local experts (when possible, the teachers in your school)
- opportunities and time for practice, reflection, and refinement

When these twenty-hour projects conclude, we love to celebrate learning with events in which students share their new skills with their peers. This celebration allows us to honour the time, effort, and learning process students undertook to attain their skills and provides an authentic audience with whom our students can share their learning. We find this further motivates students to share from the heart.

DELVE INTO YOUR CURIOSITIES

Delving into curiosities allows students to learn about topics they've wondered about but never had a chance to explore in school. These inquiries usually stem from a provocation we've set up or an observation station we've created in class to invite learners to dive into something they are curious about.

Delving into curiosities allows students to learn about topics they've wondered about but never had a chance to explore in school.

We enjoy supporting our learners in various ways as they explore their wonderings. Students might keep an inquiry journal, and every week we prompt them to free write on topics and questions they are curious about. We also go on *curiosity walks*. Students travel with a bag or knapsack to collect nature items stirring their interest. We enjoy having magnifying glasses for students to investigate their discoveries more closely. Students can also make observations, jot down notes, sketch drawings, and record their thoughts in a small journal. When we return from our adventure, we often have a sharing circle and invite learners to tell about something they discovered, something they observed, something they noticed, or something provoking their curiosity. We find that creating opportunities for learners to discover and explore their curiosities leads to meaningful and rich inquiry experiences.

As we get to know our learners throughout the year, we witness particular curiosities surface from their learning and our time together in school. We love watching our learners interact and share their wonderings with one another. We often note their curiosities, looking for patterns and areas of heightened interest to lead to more meaningful inquiries in the future. These observations help us plan learning experiences, resource selection, and our partnerships in the school.

One such curiosity surfaced in Kelli Meredith's classroom, a teacher at Gordon Head Middle School:

Recently our class delved into our curiosities as an inquiry project. One student in particular made the entire experience completely worth it. His essential question was, "How can I learn to code a video game my classmates could access and play??"

This student had always been interested in technology and the basics of coding but hadn't gone much further with it. He also struggled in most other subjects and had trouble concentrating and keeping organized. Additionally, he had some social difficulties with others in our class. He was bullied and often felt like an outsider regardless of interventions and support.

As he worked on his inquiry, he constantly looked up videos and other information about how to best develop his game and make alternate and more challenging levels. I had not seen this learner so focused all year! His one essential question led to so many other amazing questions!

When it was his turn to present what he had learned, the class went to the computer lab, where he had his game accessible through a link so everyone could play it at the same time. He was unbelievably excited as his peers logged on, played his game, and began talking, commenting, laughing, and cheering when they made it through a difficult part of his game. Seeing the look on his face and positive feedback he rarely received from his peers was so incredible that it brought tears to my eyes!

TAKE ON A NEW CHALLENGE

Taking on a new challenge can be extremely empowering for learners. Our goal in this pillar is to encourage our learners to design, problem-solve, and create. At times our learners work to solve a community problem such as supporting a food drive or helping to clean up a park. Other times they take on a design challenge using our 3D printer or drafting and designing prototypes. Whatever the challenge, students are excited and motivated by them.

We love rolling out science, technology, engineering, arts, and math (STEAM) problem-solving challenges to our students in which we can focus on STEAM. These empower our learners to inquire in different ways than they have before. It's exciting to watch them research how to solve the proposed challenge and then design and create a prototype either to answer our posed question or to present a solution to the problem they face.

We love to use our school's 3D printer with older students, who work in pairs on a design challenge we give them. The first phase of the challenge asks students to design and print *something of interest*—anything we agree is appropriate and achievable given our time and budget constraints. Typically students create whistles, various stands for their personal items, containers, clips, hooks, or other knickknacks. During this phase, they grasp some of the STEAM skills needed to succeed with our digital tools, and they acquire the experience and understanding to guide them through the rest of the challenge.

We introduce the second phase of the challenge with *Project Daniel*, a short YouTube video about the work of Mike Ebeling. A few years ago Mike traveled to war-torn Sudan to design and print

Project Daniel

prosthetics for youth who had lost limbs. Use the QR code to watch it now.

Students are challenged to design and print something to *impact someone else*. The tone and energy in the room changes dramatically. As students identify an authentic problem and design a solution to it, they become more committed and collaborative in achieving their goal. The tone in the room is more sober as their focus shifts to helping others. We've witnessed amazing creations stem from this process, including fidget spinners, adaptive tools for students with fine motor skill challenges, and an attempt at a water filtration and purification system. By shifting learners' focus to impacting others, our challenge inquiry becomes more relevant and meaningful to them. If you have a 3D printer in your school, consider trying this!

Younger students also benefit from taking on a challenge. A great example surfaced recently when we spent time with a kindergarten class looking at natural movement versus applied force movement, a common science curricular understanding at this grade level. Our goal was to provoke questions in our learners through their observations about how things move. One provocation we used was a video demonstrating the force of the wind. Students were so excited we knew we needed to explore further.

So we launched a kite design, construction, and flight inquiry. Our teacher librarian pulled all the books containing kites or images of kites for our learners to explore, and we also watched various tutorials. Students made lists of types of designs and materials used and different ways to fly a kite, and we grouped students based on the style of kite they were designing. This helped us locate materials and plan activities to ensure that everyone was supported and successful as they executed their prototype. Each group designed a kite, and each individual built a personal model to test through experimentation.

They collaborated, communicated, designed, built, observed, and revised their plans countless times. The skills and understanding students gained during these experiences were powerful. Consider trying this with your learners!

#INQUIRYMINDSET IN ACTION

The Four Pillars of Inquiry chapter provided several resources to support you in helping students tap into their passions, their goals, their curiosities, and some new challenges. Whether it be *Caine's Arcade*, Josh Kaufman, or *Project Daniel*, we challenge you to put one of these resources into action. Try it out with your students and be sure to share how they responded to our *#InquiryMindset* community.

THE ROLE OF
QUESTIONS IN INQUIRY

Beyond building the characteristics of the inquiry teacher outlined earlier, the most powerful shift you can make to adopt inquiry into your practice is to begin learning with a question. Whether it's yours or your students', questions plant the seeds for deeper inquiry to occur. Questions are the heart of the inquiry classroom and the foundation of the inquiry mindset we are nurturing in our learners.

Great ideas start with a question.

Questions spur curiosity, wonderment, and student voice and opinion. They immediately engage learners and create relevance by calling on students to access prior knowledge and understanding. Questions should be used at all levels of our educational organizations:

- teachers guiding students through learning and inquiry
- learning coaches supporting professional learning communities (PLCs) and teachers through collaborative inquiry
- principals or administrators leading staff in setting school, grade-level, and team goals
- district principals or superintendents creating an organization's growth plan and goals for individuals and institutions at all levels of the district

The power of student agency, and the opportunities this control over learning affords, extends to anyone learning in inquiry. We encourage everyone, from the classroom to the board office, to begin the learning journey with a question.

But which questions lead to meaningful research and deep learning? Are all questions worthy of our time and attention? How do we construct questions and nurture question-creating skills to empower our learners? How can we build questions to connect with our curriculum and guide lesson and unit design? What balance can we strike between modelling questions for our youngest learners and opening up the classroom for students to explore their own wonderings? This chapter sheds light on these ideas, addresses why essential questions are critical in the inquiry classroom, and outlines some amazing tools we use to support learners.

 Questions spur curiosity, wonderment, and student voice and opinion. They immediately engage learners and create relevance by calling on students to access prior knowledge and understanding.

WHAT ARE ESSENTIAL QUESTIONS?

As we shared in *Dive into Inquiry*, two resources in particular have strengthened our own understanding of the essential question process and provided us with tools we use daily to support our students to become strong creators of essential questions. They are *Essential Questions: Opening Doors to Student Understanding* by Jay McTighe and Grant Wiggins and *Make Just One Change: Teach Students to Ask Their Own Questions* by Dan Rothstein and Luz Santana. Both of these books provide context, connections, and examples we have found invaluable in transforming our classrooms into inquiry-based learning communities. Based on these books and our own experiences, we have gathered a few characteristics of essential questions that we use with our students to help create a common understanding eventually enabling them to draft their own questions.

A Strong Essential Question Must Be Open Ended

Essential questions are not answered with a quick Google search. We actually love to call essential questions *un-Googleable*. Essential questions also cannot be answered in a single lesson or in discussion with a friend. They do not have a single answer, and, in fact, the answer to an essential question may change over time because our understandings may change as we unpack different resources. As such, they require higher-order thinking such as analysis, inference, evaluation, and prediction and over time, may raise additional questions and inspire further inquiry.

Challenge your students to ask big questions, *un-Googleable* questions, questions that cannot be answered by looking in the back of the book. Great things will happen.

A Strong Essential Question Must Provide the Depth of Study Demanded by Our Course and Grade Level

We must ensure that an essential question is worthy of our course, our grade level, and our time. An essential question in a fifth-grade science unit should be quite different from an essential question in a first-grade math unit. The course and grade level will shape how thought-provoking and intellectually engaging each essential question must be and determine our students' demonstration of understanding.

A Strong Essential Question Must Be Meaningful to the Student

Essential questions must be relevant and authentic to the learner. The Four Pillars of Inquiry will ensure that this occurs. Ask your students, "How is this essential question meaningful to you?" Their responses will likely be rich, personal, and engaging. We also encourage students to share why their essential question is meaningful to them when they publicly share their work at the conclusion of our Free Inquiry unit. Their reflections always hook their audience and create a shared excitement for their inquiry.

In our classroom, students have to think critically to answer an essential question. Instead of simply looking up answers, they conduct research, participate in learning experiences, talk to one another, and create an original answer. We post the following characteristics in our classroom to remind students what their essential question should achieve:

Your essential question . . .

- should provoke deep thought
- should solicit information-gathering and evaluation of data
- should result in an original answer
- should help students conduct problem-related research
- should produce original ideas rather than predetermined answers
- should encourage critical thinking, not just memorization of facts
- may not have an answer

Using question stems is a great way for students to draft essential questions. Stems such as *Which one? How? What if? Should? Why?* evoke different types of information.

What if questions are hypothetical questions asking learners to use the knowledge they have to pose a hypothesis and consider options.

Should questions ask students to make a moral or practical decision based on evidence.

Why questions ask learners to understand and consider cause and effect. They help them understand relationships and get to the essence of an issue.

We also post these longer stems in our classroom and refer to them often:

- How would you...?
- What would result if...?
- How would you describe...?
- How does...compare with...?
- What is the relationship between...and...?
- What would happen if...?
- How could you change...?
- How would you improve...?
- How do you feel about...?
- Why do you believe...?
- What is your opinion of...?
- What choice would you have made?
- What would you do differently?
- Why do you feel...?
- How would you go about solving...?
- If you were in this position, what would you do?
- Why do/don't you support...?
- What could improve about...?

From time to time, we ask students to use these longer stems to draft their own essential questions we can discuss together, in small groups and as a class. This allows us to assess how adept learners are becoming in asking rich and compelling questions.

THE ROLE OF CLOSED QUESTIONS
IN INQUIRY

Closed questions have gotten a bad reputation in the inquiry world for many reasons. Whether because they don't lead to deep learning, they're *Googleable*, they tend to be content focused (and easily standardized when it comes to assessment), or they don't drive powerful inquiry, *closed* questions have become synonymous with *bad* questions.

But this shouldn't be the case.

Closed questions are *necessary* in learning. They provide a common understanding of subject matter, allowing learners to collaborate and create new, and often personalized, meaning. They provide the jargon—language allowing users to speak intelligently, engagingly, persuasively, and confidently—of a discipline or focus area. Additionally, closed questions are the first step in the research phase of inquiry; we propose that these must be answered to explore deep learning and open questions.

 Closed questions are *necessary* in learning. They open powerful doors for learners to collaborate and create new personalized meaning.

For example, literature students cannot discuss how stories are important and powerful vehicles of change without understanding literary tools such as point of view, metaphor, symbolism, voice, and so forth. Likewise, learners in a history classroom cannot explore how injustices in history can be justified depending on one's perspective without understanding, at least on the surface, the causes and key players in several historical turmoils.

HOW TO FOSTER A CULTURE OF QUESTIONS

The inquiry teacher aims to create a classroom fostering a culture of questions. These questions, wonderings, and curiosities drive learning, determine resources and artifacts, and guide us as we support our students. Our learners need to understand that questions are the root of learning and that their own wonderings will be honoured and cultivated in the classroom. Long before students experience Free Inquiry, we create this culture of questions through numerous methods, activities, and artifacts. All of these promote the same outcome: providing our learners with the time and space to explore questions and with the understanding that questions have a powerful place in our classroom.

 Our learners need to understand that questions are the root of learning and that their own wonderings will be honoured and cultivated in the classroom.

Nadine McIntyre of Ecole Deep Cove Elementary agrees. She daily models her own questions for her students so they can see the importance of questions in learning.

To foster this culture of questioning in my classroom, I spend a great deal of time modelling and sharing my own

wonders. It's important for my learners to know I don't have all the answers—I'm on my own learning journey just as they are. I honour all of my students' questions and wonders to show they are an integral part of our learning. No matter the topic, learning activity, or direction my learners guide our inquiry, their open-ended questions help deepen our learning. Finding these moments where my students' voices can shine creates a culture of questioning in our classroom.

As we break down some of the resources and activities we've used to foster this culture of questions, we hope you can find some to adopt into your own practice.

THE QUESTION FORMULATION TECHNIQUE

We find one of the most powerful additions to our practice to help foster a culture of questions is our use of the Question Formulation Technique (QFT) as outlined in *Make Just One Change: Teach Students to Ask Their Own Questions.* The QFT is an evidence-based strategy for improving students' ability to formulate *their own* questions. All too often in the traditional classroom setting, it is the teacher's questions that shape lessons and learning opportunities. The QFT flips this control around to the learner and empowers students to hone their question-creation skills, skills that draw on them to summarize, analyze, and evaluate questions that *they've* constructed.

We use the QFT in a scaffolded manner throughout the school year. During the earlier months and with our younger learners, we model the process and demonstrate our own thinking aloud on our classroom projector or whiteboard. Students observe how we go through the QFT steps and create new and exciting questions along the way. When the opportunity naturally arises, we include student voice and participation in this activity until, over time, students are ready to embark on the QFT in pairs or as individuals.

To truly realize the power of the QFT, you should explore the Right Question Institute and their resource pages (rightquestion. org). As you continue reading this chapter, consider how you can pair the inquiry tools we propose with what you learn of the QFT. We are confident you'll love what you discover!

THE CLOSED-QUESTION "WORKSHEET"

After an inquiry topic has been selected (by the teacher or the student), we love students to brainstorm closed questions for five minutes. We provide only five minutes because students enjoy the challenge of getting as many questions as they can within a time limit. Next they prioritize these *must-know* questions from the most to the least critical. If younger learners struggle with the idea of *must-know*, we model it. Other times we may prompt students to prioritize questions or wonderings in terms of personal interest and relevance.

This activity helps students identify and create the first phase in their inquiry—researching and answering these questions—and guides our next steps toward locating information and resources. Essentially, these closed questions are the foundation of their learning and provide the jargon and common understanding to enable them to dig deeper into their inquiry.

Differentiation surfaces as students target their own *need-to-know* information, and this is powerful. This agency over learning sets the tone for deeper inquiry to occur—one of confidence and control receiving the support and expertise of the inquiry teacher.

We have sarcastically titled this activity the Closed-Question "Worksheet." The term *worksheet* has a negative connotation, hinting at passive and unimportant learning; however, as you can see, this activity is not passive or unimportant. Learners have actively created the questions and subsequently identified relevance in them. Everything teachers dislike about worksheets is curbed in this activity. Plus, we have found that students truly enjoy researching and answering these questions; they get excited working through the *worksheet*, sharing information, and exploring resources to support their journey. When they answer their own questions, they are rewarded by a sense of discovery that builds confidence and hones valuable research and exploration skills.

Scaffold as necessary for your own classroom by doing this activity as a group, putting all student questions on a poster board or Google Doc *worksheet*. Students can then select, as individuals or in pairs, a question to research and share with the group. This scaffolding will help model the process for our younger learners while simultaneously building the foundation for inquiry.

THE CURIOSITY JAR

The Curiosity Jar is a powerful tool to help learners grasp that their questions matter, and it is one of our favourite ways to foster a culture of questions in our classroom. Students write a question, wondering, or curiosity and put it into the jar—typically an extra-large, student-decorated jar. Periodically, the teacher uses a question from the jar as a teaching tool. We've seen this done in a number of engaging ways—Carpet Time, Living Library, Library Time, Shaping Learning—yielding powerful results.

Carpet Time

You can pull out questions during carpet time and ask students a series of prompts to help them access prior knowledge, make connections to others' questions, and pinpoint resources to help answer the questions. Typically you would pre-read the questions to formulate a plan and approach to the discussion. Discussion prompts might include questions like these:

- Has anyone ever wondered the same thing? Tell us about your wondering.
- Does anyone know anything to help us answer this question?
- Has anyone ever read or watched anything possibly helpful with this question?
- If we needed to do some research, what could we do to get help with this question? Where could we go? Who would we ask?
- Does this question connect with something we've been learning about in class or something you've learned at home?
- Does anyone have a friend or relative who could help us with this curiosity?

You can also use available technology to research questions with the class in real time. For example, show students a YouTube video you've previewed to answer, *How do you build an igloo?* Or take them to NASA's online education resources to learn more about, *How do the planets in our solar system differ from one another?* This allows learners to become more familiar with researching while reinforcing what constitutes a valuable and valid source.

Through this activity, students witness you using their wondering, honouring their curiosity through asking classmates for their thoughts, and finally, locating and researching rich information online to deepen understanding. It's powerful stuff!

Living Library

Call on parents of your students, colleagues within your schools, community members or business people, or your online PLN to help answer questions from the Curiosity Jar. When we give the responsibility of sharing information to our network, students begin to understand that learning isn't a top-down model with you being in sole possession of knowledge. Information can be accessed through a variety of rich sources, and, in this situation, the teacher becomes a facilitator of locating information.

Imagine how meaningful it would be for a student's question to be answered by a classmate's parents, another staff member, a fireman, a pharmacist, or a pilot. Reaching out to your PLN with a *call to action* demonstrates how social media can transform learning and can be used in a powerful, respectful, and responsible way. We often tweet out questions from our Curiosity Jar and are pleasantly surprised when people share and respond to our requests. We never know who will respond or where they'll take our queries but, more often than not, we have an exciting learning experience.

Library Time

Pass the Curiosity Jar to your teacher librarian and have these *inquiry allies* use the students' questions to shape research activities and locate and gather information in the library. Teacher librarians preview the questions and pull relevant books from the library shelves and display them for students to browse. They can also encourage students to try to locate a few other books connecting to their curiosity, which calls on learners to use another powerful research skill: skimming. This tends to be an engaging experience, as learners typically pair off and share the books they've discovered in a comfortable space in the library by reflecting on *how do you know the book(s) you've selected relate to your question?* Students can sign out these titles and read to deepen their understanding of their wondering.

Shaping Learning

Use questions from the Curiosity Jar as a springboard to other plans for learning in your classroom. Using the wonderings from a carpet discussion, you can make connections to other parts of the curriculum. For example, the igloo curiosity just mentioned could tie to further learning about ecosystems and habitats in science or culture and history in social studies. The NASA example could be tied to science objectives and math outcomes. Both questions also lend well to furthering literacy development through reading books learners check out from our library. The ties across our curriculum clearly and meaningfully surface through this activity. Relevance is clarified, and opportunities for cross-curricular learning present themselves. For younger students, we often plan our Structured and Controlled units of study by using the Curiosity Jar as a springboard for our lesson and unit design.

THE WONDER WALL

The Wonder Wall is a dedicated space where students can post their wonderings, questions, and curiosities in a visible and collective manner. Like the Curiosity Jar, the Wonder Wall is another activity we use in inspiring ways to empower learners by showing them that their questions matter and their voices can shape learning in our classroom.

In the Classroom

By providing a Wonder Wall in our classrooms, we demonstrate the importance of student questions in our shared learning space.

Students record their wonderings, post them to the Wonder Wall, and are then given support to deepen their understanding of their query. This process helps create an inquiry mindset, which values questions as the starting point of learning, honours student voice, and encourages creativity and agency in the classroom.

In our primary classrooms, we take photos of each student, prompting them to strike a "deeply curious" pose. We print and laminate the images and post them along a wall. When possible we love to provide the entire length of a classroom so students visualize the importance of their questions and the magnitude of their voice. We add a laminated thought bubble to each image to give the impression that their wonderings are on display for all to see. Students are encouraged to write their question in their thought bubble as a commitment to explore it further. When they're finished researching and deepening understanding, or a new wondering surfaces, students simply erase their question and write a new one in its place. As you can see in the photo from Rebecca's wall, you can participate as well by including your own photo and wondering on the wall.

As with the Curiosity Jar, you can use these questions to demonstrate research pathways. Students could discover, for example, how to locate and select rich and valid resources, how to access our living library, how to further collaborate with our teacher librarian, and how to shape learning in the classroom.

Students love this large version of the Wonder Wall. They enjoy looking at their classmates' wonderings and talking about them together. They bring their own thoughts, personalities, and understandings to each other's questions and, in doing so, become active contributors in the learning process as opposed to passive consumers. Students get excited when new wonderings are written or when the teacher explores their queries in class. These discussions act as

Rebecca Bathurst-Hunt, George Jay Elementary

seeds to create lifelong learners—students who grasp their role in the inquiry classroom from a young age.

Wonder Repositories

Wonder Repositories are a personalized twist on the Wonder Wall but with the same goal: to create a space where student curiosities and wonderings can be housed and later explored more deeply. The power of Wonder Repositories is that students have their own private bucket or bag to store their wonderings in. Writing, images, artwork, artifacts, and tokens of their imaginings are all items learners love to add. Students decorate their buckets and bags, a meaningful art activity when paired with a prompt such as *when you close your eyes and think on a wondering, what shines through? What colours do you see?* The resulting beauty and personalization demonstrated is amazing!

Students can add items to their bags and buckets at any time, and you can provide prompts and provocations to encourage the process. We suggest that learners also keep a wonder journal—a notepad to jot down their thoughts—in their buckets and bags. Opportunities to pull out these notepads and artifacts to help shape learning, inform instruction, and aid in assessment are plentiful. Whether these wonderings are used in Show and Share as an oral language assessment or as a writing prompt to aid in a writing proficiency assessment, students always speak more engagingly and write more beautifully when the focus is something they're interested in and curious about.

Wonder Prompts

Wonder Prompts can be used to encourage writing about objects from students' Wonder Repositories or to encourage imaginative writing, creativity, and exploration of student wonderings. Try using one prompt or put up a few and allow students to pick the one most inspiring to them.

- Where do you think this object came from?
- What do you think this object is made of?
- Who do you think would use this object, and in what different ways might it be used?
- Why do you think this object was invented?
- What do you think would happen if part of this object were missing? Could it be used for something else?
- Why do you think this object is part of our natural environment? What is its role?
- What do you think happens after we use this object? Where does it go? How does it decompose?
- Focus on this object. What different parts of the object do you notice?

- If you could look at your object through a powerful magnifying glass, what do you imagine you would see and discover on this object?
- What do you think might happen to this object if it gets wet?
- What do you imagine would happen to this object if sat in the sun or a warm spot too long?
- How do you think we would have used this object fifty years ago?
- How does this object move? Do you think it can move naturally, or does it require an applied force to move?
- How could this object help others? What might it help them do?
- How do you think animals would use this object?
- Will this object still be around in ten years? Where do you think it might be found? Will it still be useful?
- What other uses do you think people might have for this object?
- What would you see if you climbed to the top of the tree in the playground?
- What do you think our school used to look like fifty years ago?
- When you look outside the window, what do you see? What would happen to this area if a storm came through? What type of storm would it be?
- What would you see if you went deep sea scuba diving?
- Imagine you are a bird; what would you see if you flew over our town?
- Imagine sitting in a rocket ship; what would it feel like to blast off?

- What do you think it would be like to ride with the checked luggage on a plane?
- Imagine you are in the middle of the rainforest; what do you hear?
- How do you think rainbows are made?
- Why do you think it gets foggy?
- How do you think a lion would survive in the city?
- How do you think bees work together in their hive?

In the Library

In the library, the teacher librarian creates a Wonder Wall on a bulletin board where all students can post their wonderings using sticky notes. Students can post questions on their own accord or when a question arises during a visit and it cannot be easily answered. The teacher librarian can use these queries to guide lessons on research, locating information, and finding credible and appropriate sources. We also use these questions as a conversation starter. Pairs of students select a question, discuss it, and then see whether they can locate a book in the library connected to their query. Furthermore, the teacher librarian can focus on literacy skills such as note-taking, providing evidence for answers, and connecting and inferring skills. When these skills surface from the Wonder Wall in the library space, opportunities for students to make powerful connections are at their fingertips. Whether the skill is related to books, digital sources and databases, or the research expert in the room, they are reinforced by the relevance of the learners' questions from the Wonder Wall.

Jane Spies, a former teacher librarian at Shoreline Middle School, shares how she used the Wonder Wall in her library space:

In our library, students are welcome to write a question on a sticky and add it to our Wonder Wall whenever they feel compelled. At times students add their own questions without

me noticing; other times I hear a student ask a question requir-
ing more time to fully answer or I think other students would
be interested in it so I ask them to add those to our Wonder
Wall. Any "off topic" questions surfacing during class also get
added to our Wonder Wall to be explored at a later time, per-
haps at the end of a research unit, during Wonder Wall time in
library skills classes, or to reinforce a skill. For example, I often
use Wonder Wall questions to demonstrate asking open-ended
and closed-ended questions, locating information, or finding
credible and appropriate sources.

The questions on the library Wonder Wall are not neces-
sarily related to one topic; they cover a broad range of things.
The Wonder Wall allows students to become experts on a topic
and deepen learning in an authentic way. For example, each
year my students teach their parents the difference between
open-ended and close-ended questions during student-led
conferences. Parents and students create questions together
for the Wonder Wall—some profound, others silly and hilar-
ious, and some questions they truly want answers to. Seeing
students and parents engaged in the simple activity of asking
questions is amazing. It's a fantastic way for them to learn
more about each other in a safe, fun, engaging, and meaning-
ful way.

At some point, students want answers to the Wonder Wall
questions. Before I set them off to explore resources, deepen
learning, and find answers, I remind them about the impor-
tance of connecting to a question, where and how to gather
information in our library space, the importance of asking
more questions to further understanding, and relying on
prior knowledge to infer answers to any new questions. The
Wonder Wall gives students a chance to practice and transfer

the inquiry skills they have learned in class using their own questions. Interestingly, I've noticed often the seemingly silliest questions lead to some of the deepest and most exciting learning!

Jane Spies at Shoreline School

Online

We love creating a *virtual* Wonder Wall—an online space allowing students to share their questions with their classmates while simultaneously solidifying their understanding of digital citizenship. Our most quiet and introverted students find this option extremely empowering. They don't get overwhelmed by their peers' voices, they can take the time to reflect and craft their wondering before they post it, and they feel much more confident than if they were asked to use the collaborative Wonder Wall in the classroom or library. Following are a few online tools and platforms that we absolutely love. All of these are intuitive, collaborative, and free.

Flipgrid

Flipgrid is a video-response platform in which you and your students post topics, record responses to prompts, and reply and collaborate with their peers. Flipgrid is one of our favourite platforms for making students' voices heard and their thinking visible. It's easy to use and fosters confidence and ownership over sharing understanding. Teachers can easily and safely send student responses to parents as evidence of learning, creating a virtual window into what happens inside the classroom from day to day. We've found it extremely powerful to seamlessly connect with parents and students and witness the impact of our collaboration and sharing. The paid Flipgrid version offers another advantage in that students begin to interact with their peers using the platform. They provide feedback, advice, and insight into one another's wonderings and, before we know it, a learning community has surfaced—one in which the teacher isn't the sole conduit of deepening understanding. Rather, a partnership between teacher and students now drives learning.

Answer Garden

Answer Garden is a powerful text-focused interface allowing you to pin prompts for your class and students to post their ideas and opinions to the prompts. Students simply type in their thoughts and submit them to this collaborative space where all entries are collated. A great feature of Answer Garden is that student voice is shared to the class in real time, allowing the audience to see their peers' unique opinions as well as opinions they may share. Entries submitted by multiple students are displayed in a larger font size, reflecting the support from the class for a common opinion. You can even save the visual word cloud for reference later in learning. We love using these saved images to reflect on how our wonderings have changed and on new opinions and understandings we have formed. Additionally, having students speak or write as part of this reflection activity is a highly relevant and personally meaningful process.

Padlet

Padlet is a platform allowing you to create a virtual blank digital wall where you can gather student voice, answers, and opinions in a visual format. You can go beyond a text prompt and include documents, images, video, and music as provocations and wonderings to stir interest and inspire students. You can easily share these collaborative digital walls with an audience of parents, other teachers, or your PLN. We love using Padlet as a virtual pinboard of our collective wonderings on a prompt based on one of the Four Pillars of Inquiry. Students can make connections with their peers on the wall by connecting similarities or common interests, ideas, and passions. The surfacing learning community is powerful thanks to the ease of use Padlet provides as well as the agency fostered by learners having more control over the sharing and publishing process.

Recap

Recap is a powerful question-and-answer platform seamlessly providing your classroom with an ecosystem to share wonderings and collaborate with one another. You post a prompt (we love posting short videos called the Journey), and students respond with their own questions or wonderings. Each student question creates an extension from the Journey and provides space and structure for their peers to reply and even post their own video response. A slick feature is that the character limit on text replies to another's wonderings is quite high, allowing students to leave a detailed and meaningful reply to whatever questions spark their interests.

Collectively these tools afford fantastic opportunities to broaden research and deepen understanding. First, you can easily share these with parents and other family members who could provide praise, advice, and support. We often email our Weekly Wonderings to parents within our class newsletter so they get a glimpse of the connections their sons and daughters are making in the classroom. During Parent Night, whether it's student led or teacher led, you can share these platforms as evidence of learning. When parents see more than their child's writing—perhaps a video reflection or a recorded wondering—they gain a more detailed and personalized picture of where their child is in their learning and where we need to go next.

Second, we love to tweet out these digital wonderings to our PLN and call on them to support our learners in the exploration of their wonderings. We are always pleasantly surprised by who responds—from astronauts to politicians to celebrities to sports heroes—and where our sharing takes us, but we are convinced that sharing wonderings on Twitter has huge potential. Naturally, students witness the impact of social media when it's used to create new understandings and experiences.

Third, digital literacy skills are reinforced when we collaborate in our virtual Wonder Wall. Becoming competent adopters of tech, users of a platform, and contributors to an interface at a young age with the support and guidance of a teacher creates a foundation for strong lifelong digital literacy skills.

Using these tools—or others of your own—you can generate many open-ended questions. Once a question is created, whether it's the teacher's or it stems from a wondering or curiosity from students, it's time to explore and research the inquiry more deeply.

#INQUIRYMINDSET IN ACTION

In this chapter, we outlined a range of powerful ways to help you create a culture of questions in your classroom, including the Curiosity Jar, the Wonder Wall, the Closed-Question "Worksheet," and the QFT. We also offered several online tools such as Flipgrid, Padlet, Answer Garden, and Recap. Select any one of these empowering tools and put them into action in your classroom. Share a photo of a curiosity, a wonder, a Closed-Question "Worksheet," or a question created in the QFT. Share a video from Flipgrid, a link to your Padlet, a photo of your Answer Garden, or a journey from your Recap. Whatever you decide, please be sure to share it to our *#InquiryMindset* community.

EXPLORE AND RESEARCH: THE TEACHER LIBRARIAN AS AN INQUIRY ALLY

Creating critical thinkers and mindful researchers is a huge benefit of adopting an inquiry approach to learning. In our increasingly connected world in which technology has accelerated the ease of locating and accessing information, our learners face challenges like no generation before them in terms of needing to assess content and determine whether a source of information is valid, needed, and helpful. To best prepare them to grapple with a seemingly infinite number of websites and sources of digital media, educators must teach learners exploration and research skills. And the most powerful partner a teacher can have is the teacher librarian.

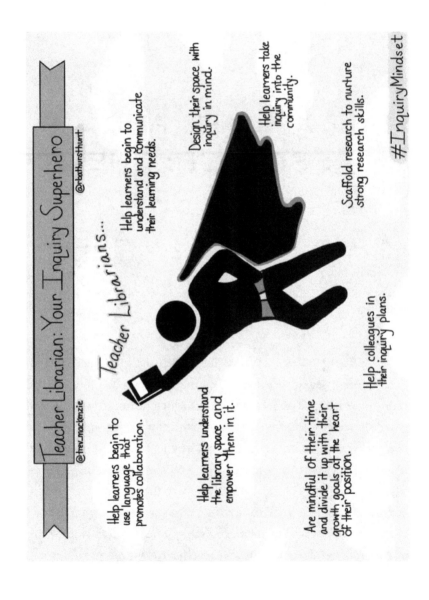

Teacher Librarian: Your Inquiry Superhero

@trev.mackenzie   @rbathursthurst

Teacher Librarians...

Help learners begin to use language that promotes collaboration.

Help learners understand the library space and empower them in it.

Help learners begin to understand and communicate their learning needs.

Design their space with inquiry in mind.

Help learners take inquiry into the community.

Scaffold research to nurture strong research skills.

Are mindful of their time and divide it up with their growth goals at the heart of their position.

Help colleagues in their inquiry plans.

#InquiryMindset

The most powerful partner a teacher can have in their inquiry journey is the teacher librarian.

Gone are the days of the *ssh-h-h-h* library, traditionally a space where learning was an isolated activity, consisting mostly of locating a book and reading with a librarian or quietly to oneself. Today's library resembles a learning commons, a lively space where collaboration and support in learning are the norm. In libraries we've visited, we've witnessed opportunities for learners to access online resources, receive tutoring support, collaborate with peers (even across grade groupings), create content, hold meetings, and even read and study! These spaces include a diverse array of learning tools beyond hard resources and books; they're full of digital equipment, makerspaces, and publishing services, providing learners with ample opportunity to create rather than merely consume.

And today's teacher librarian is the facilitator of these learning commons. Teacher librarians are highly skilled in identifying a challenge, planning a learning pathway, and providing the necessary support for goals to be attained. These educators encourage collaboration, facilitate proficient research, and support accessing online information. They have a finger on the pulse of tech trends and how to best support our learners in acquiring and assessing information. We love our teacher librarians!

One of the most critical jobs of primary teacher librarians is teaching our youngest learners how to properly collaborate and communicate with other learners. They teach students how to do the following:

- actively listen to peers

- assess strengths and weaknesses of someone else's perspective
- question to deepen conversation and create new understandings
- brainstorm solutions to problems
- reflect on their role in the collaboration

Teacher librarians have a finger on the pulse of tech trends and how to best support our learners in acquiring and assessing information.

These skills are the foundation for the higher-order thinking skills—analysing, evaluating, and creating—our learners will rely on more heavily later in their educational journey. These skills foster empathy and compassion for others, traits we hold dear when working with our learners.

We have discovered that teacher librarians have many powerful resources to support students as they acquire these skills.

Teacher librarians design their space with inquiry in mind.

The design of a learning commons impacts how learners use the space. If we want learners to research, collaborate, create, or be mindful, we need to provide them with specific spaces supporting each of these unique activities. Teacher librarians need to demonstrate how these spaces are used, explicitly teach learners the benefit and purpose of each space, and empower them with agency to select the space they need.

Anzac Park Public School, a highly innovative primary school in Sydney, Australia, is a powerful example of how space design supports learning. Anzac Park boasts future-focused learning spaces, a design concept allowing spaces to evolve and adapt as educational practices change. These learning spaces allow teachers and learners the flexibility to collaborate, reflect, and share. Modular furniture and the specific design of learning spaces seamlessly provide agency to the learner to reflect on individual learning needs and design or select a space best suited to the identified need.

Four learning spaces are used at Anzac Park: the cave, the watering hole, the campfire, and the mountain top. These learning spaces stem from the work of David Thorpe's *Campfires in Cyberspace*, and each is used for a different purpose. Principal Unity Taylor-Hill elaborates on the school's vision:

> At Anzac Park Public School, our aim is to create an environment where staff and students collaborate in their learning, enabling everyone to reach their potential through an innovative and negotiated curriculum that challenges and supports all members of the school community.
>
> We recognise that we need to create learning and teaching environments where the curriculum and the pedagogy reflect today's world. At Anzac Park we are committed to providing learning spaces that are designed to be configured in different ways to suit the learning needs of students. Our purposeful learning spaces enable us to place student learning at the core of our decision making. It provides opportunities for social and collaborative learning, integrated curriculum delivery, a mix of teacher-directed and student-directed teaching and learning, independent learning, project work, direct instruction, innovative and creative thinking, relationship building, and problem-solving skills.
>
> A flexible learning space design is inclusive by allowing for different learning styles and more experimentation. It allows students and teachers to move more seamlessly through

different kinds of learning spaces, both physical and virtual, by ensuring that the environment remains flexible. Our focus on flexible learning spaces at Anzac Park allows teachers to construct and adapt the learning to meet the needs of students, to personalise instruction, and allow students to explore different models of learning.

At Anzac Park, we have implemented futurist David Thornburg's archetypal learning environments to guide our learning space policy. These metaphors allow students to actively consider the type of learning that is required for each lesson and how the physical space needs to alter to meet the learning taking place. These archetypes are actively taught to students so that our students have an understanding of the different learning behaviours required for each of the archetypes.

Let's take a closer look at these metaphors now:

The Cave is a private space where an individual can think, reflect, and transform learning from external knowledge to internal understandings. It is a place for independent work, reflection, and self-assessment. Learners use the cave when they need a quiet space to work, when they require some time to be undisturbed, and when they want to stay on task. Nooks, corner spaces, single desks, or computer workstations all are part of the design of the cave.

The Watering Hole is an informal space where peers can share information and discoveries, acting as both learner and teacher simultaneously. The watering hole is a space for ideas and the promotion of a shared understanding. It is for collaborative group time. Learners use the watering hole when they want to work with a team and share and listen to others' opinions. Everyone contributes in this space. Circular tables, furniture designed for groups, or anything resembling a station for collaboration can be found here.

The Campfire is a space where people gather to learn from an expert. The experts are not only teachers but also students who are empowered to share their learning with peers and teachers. Larger gatherings such as class meetings, talking circles, class sharing, debate, or other class-wide activities occur at the Campfire. In this space, learners focus on being active listeners, responding to questions, and respecting the voice of their peers when others are sharing.

Life is a space designed to support the application of knowledge and is an essential component of the learning process. When we learn something in anticipation of its immediate use, we not only reinforce our own understanding, we also increase the likelihood that what we are learning will not be forgotten.

Learners are encouraged to reflect on their learning needs, redesign the room to suit these needs, and further reflect and adapt *as they learn*. This is a great example of how design not only supports agency but also empowers inquiry. Students experience a spiral of learning continuously supporting metacognition, ownership, and responsibility over their role in the classroom. The result is the fostering of the inquiry mindset that inquiry teachers strive for. From books to digital tools to diverse spaces, Anzac Park's use of Thorpe's archetypal learning environments marries design with the heart of the learning commons—a space to learn, collaborate, and create.

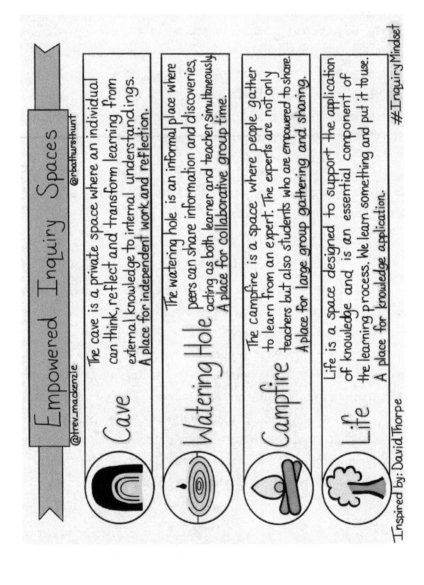

Empowered Inquiry Spaces

@trev.mackenzie   @rbathursthunt

Cave
The cave is a private space where an individual can think, reflect and transform learning from external knowledge to internal understandings. A place for independent work and reflection.

Watering Hole
The watering hole is an informal place where peers can share information and discoveries, acting as both learner and teacher simultaneously. A place for collaborative group time.

Campfire
The campfire is a space where people gather to learn from an expert. The experts are not only teachers but also students who are empowered to share. A place for large group gathering and sharing.

Life
Life is a space designed to support the application of knowledge and is an essential component of the learning process. We learn something and put it to use. A place for knowledge application.

Inspired by: David Thorpe   #InquiryMindset

 Student agency is more than merely providing options for assignments. It's about empowering learners to truly understand *what* they need and *how* they can have these needs met.

Teacher librarians help learners understand and communicate their learning needs.

Students who can reflect on their learning, as opposed to merely focusing on the learning target, become stronger inquiry students later in their educational journey. When students can consider the process by which they interact with the world around them, they learn to understand and communicate their learning needs. Teacher librarians can support students in their development of these skills in a number of ways:

- Read picture and story books reflecting mindfulness, perseverance, and teamwork, as well as creativity, imagination, and divergent thinking. We love Andrea Beaty's books, because they inspire young learners to take risks with their thinking, go forth with their questions, and celebrate their learning. Our favourites from Andrea are *Rosie Revere, Engineer; Ava Twist, Scientist;* and *Iggy Peck, Architect.* Some of our other favourite picture and story books are:

    What Do You Do with an Idea? by Kobi Yamada

    The Most Magnificent Thing by Ashley Spires

    I Wonder by Annaka Harris

    Beautiful Oops! by Barney Saltzberg

    Not A Box by Antoinette Portis

Flotsam by David Wiesner

When I Build with Blocks by Niki Alling

- Tell them stories of your own learning experiences and provide tips on how to reflect. When you share personal anecdotes, talking students through their thinking, learners can visualize *how* you learn. To scaffold your sharing and support your learners, use stems such as . . .

   I was thinking that...

   What I wondered was...

   My thinking made me believe that...

- Give students some sentence stems of their own to help them verbalize their thoughts and needs. Display them and help learners rehearse them through conversation and role play.

- Discuss and demonstrate the process of creating something. Show learners each step and how these steps lead to a more refined product. Consider showing them what happens when one of these steps is missed, taken out, or forgotten. This helps learners grasp the importance of process and reflection in a clear and tangible manner.

- Create learning opportunities using a diverse array of resources to help students interact with all forms of information and understand which forms impact and deepen their understanding the most. Use text, video, images, guest speakers, artifacts, music, and so forth.

Teacher librarians help learners use language promoting collaboration.

Verbal communication *and* active listening skills are both part of collaboration. Teacher librarians can impact how confident learners are working with others by supporting them to refine their language and listening skills during the early years of their education.

- Continue to read picture and story books reflecting the goals of teamwork and collaboration. Keep making connections with your own learning experiences via stories and "tips" on how to collaborate and work together. Some of our favourite titles include the following:

    Going Places by Paul A. Reynolds & Peter H. Reynolds
    Anything Is Possible by Giulia Belloni
    The Box by Axel Janssens
    The Way Back Home by Oliver Jeffers
    Art & Max by David Wiesner
    Pumpkin Soup by Helen Cooper

- Display and rehearse collaboration using active listening sentence stems to deepen learning, enhance partnership, and help students grasp their role in collaboration. Display stems and encourage learners to rehearse using them through conversation and role play. Here are a few stems we love using with learners:

    You feel...
    I heard you say...
    Tell me more about...

Teacher librarians help learners understand the library space and empower them in it.

The design of our library space impacts how our learners interact with one another as well as with the resources and experiences in the space. Being mindful of what these spaces look like, how they're used, and what intentions we have behind them are important items to consider when empowering our learners.

The design of our library space impacts how our learners interact with one another as well as with the resources and experiences in the space.

- Books are important, but shift the main focus of the library away from books and onto *experiences*. Add a provocation table, a poetry centre, a Wonder Wall, and flexible furniture as well as visual cues, sentence stems, and supports to guide learners in how the space can be used. Create flow from space to space so learners can seamlessly explore, interact, and discover rich learning experiences on their own.

- Weave in opportunities for school clubs to use the library space. Regardless of the group—clubs for coding, maker-space, gaming, digital art, poetry, writing, or chess—the library should be the hub of student-led interests and passions in the school. By providing a home for these learners to share their common love for something, we demonstrate that the learning commons is about more than books. It's a place where passions go to flourish through the support of the teachers in the school.

- Get your learners to help design and set up particular areas and displays in the space. Ask learners to create and display an essential question on a bulletin board and provide markers and sticky notes for students to post their observations, wonderings, and understandings about the question. Encourage learners to bring in artifacts for specific holidays and then research and select books from the space to accompany these artifacts as part of a student-created provocation table. Your students will love carving a path between school and home that impacts their peers!

Teacher librarians are mindful of their time and divide it according to their growth goals.

Set aside specific time for your partnerships with particular grade groupings. If your goal for kindergarten and grade one students is to help them better understand and communicate their learning needs, allocate the time required to meet this goal. Structure your days and weeks to ensure that you can focus on your vision and support all learners.

Earmark a small portion of your total time (consider a fifth of your week) to work solely with your youngest learners: kindergarten and grade one students. This concentrated focus of time and planning allows you to invest in and help learners grow into strong collaborators and empowered students. Imagine working deeply with the same learners every week for consecutive years. Through your vision, planning, and nurturing, you ensure that these students develop the specific skills and understandings needed to be more communicative and collaborative learners.

Teacher librarians scaffold skills over years to best help learners grow over time. Their vision includes identifying goals for each grade level, outlining a plan to attain these goals, and adopting clear and focused strategies to make these goals a reality. This process combines big ideas with specific and explicit decisions around activities, resources, lessons, and teaching. Map this out for your school and your learners, brainstorm how you'll weave these ideas into your plan, and take action toward making this plan a reality!

Teacher librarians help colleagues in their inquiry plans.

Teacher librarians are not just resources for younger learners; they are also resources for our adult learners: the teachers! You can create accessible and meaningful opportunities for your colleagues to adopt inquiry in their classrooms. Helping them empower their learners strengthens the work and efforts you've made in the library by extending it into the classroom. This provides rich partnerships that help model collaboration skills for students across your school and build staff capability toward becoming the teachers our learners need.

Teacher librarians are not just resources for younger learners; they are also resources for our adult learners: the teachers!

Inquiry Bins are fun and engaging resources prepared by teacher librarians to support inquiry in the classroom. Lorraine Powell at Ecole Willows Elementary uses Inquiry Bins to engage her learners and strengthen inquiry in her school:

> We have several different Inquiry Bins, full of resources and tools connected to a specific inquiry topic, designed and created for a specific local outdoor space in our community. Teachers can sign out an Inquiry Bin, and, combined with a Structured Inquiry unit plan, it provides everything they need to create a rich inquiry experience for their learners. Guidebooks, backpacks, magnifying glasses, nets, and even contact information for local experts are found in our Inquiry Bins. We also add a binder of lesson ideas, notes, and

provocations to further support our teachers. Whether to a park, beach, forest, or field near our school, teachers can connect their inquiry to our community, plan a small excursion or curiosity walk, and invite parents to support and participate in the learning.

Plan and lead a Guided Inquiry unit in the library on a topic selected by your colleagues. Through your mindful planning and ease of access to resources, you can structure a powerful inquiry unit for your learners. Break down your topic into subtopics the group can unpack together. Students can also choose a specific subtopic to dive into more deeply.

For example, "ecosystems" lends well to a Guided Inquiry unit. The teacher librarian leads the class through some preliminary learning to help them gain an understanding of the topic as well as subtopics such as forest, grasslands, desert, tundra, and marine. The goal is to introduce the topic and subtopics enough to provide students with a clear picture so they can select a subtopic of their own to learn more about in a small group.

To help learners select a subtopic, lay out books for each one on a separate table. Prompt students to explore these resources, browse and skim a few books, sit and read one in particular for a few minutes and, eventually, select an ecosystem they'd like to learn more about in the coming days. At the end of the session, ask students to write their names on two sticky notes and leave them on the tables of the two ecosystems they're most excited about. You can then ensure that all students learn about a topic they want.

We've seen this Guided Inquiry taken a step further by asking students to research an animal of their interest inhabiting the specific ecosystem they're studying. This further strengthens the personalized thread for each learner in this Guided Inquiry unit as learners research and demonstrate understanding using an animal and ecosystem of their choice while also grasping the larger concepts of the unit.

Teacher librarians help learners take inquiry into the community.

Teacher librarians help connect inquiry in the classroom, library, and school to their surrounding community in a variety of powerful ways. Whether it's getting learners access to artifacts at a local museum, visiting a heritage site or historical monument, attending an exhibit at an art gallery, or touring government and political institutions, teacher librarians know that taking inquiry beyond the walls of our school can deepen learning and is worthy of their efforts.

Sarah McLeod, teacher librarian at Glenlyon Norfolk School, facilitates these community inquiry ties for her staff and her students through her Heritage Inquiry project. Have a read:

Heritage Inquiry—one of my all-time favourite projects for students in grades four and five—generates an inquiry question on a specific topic of personal interest about an element of our local history, geography, or heritage. To inspire students and spark discussion, we visit one of the many local museums, archives, or historical landmarks in our community. Watching other provocations, including short documentaries or videos, can also generate ideas. A noteworthy person or an event from a student's family history might also be a topic fulfilling for the student and his or her family to explore more deeply. This exposure to history engages student curiosity and allows them to explore historically significant topics.

Once topics are chosen and inquiry questions generated, I make students aware of the resources available to help with their research. At this early stage of research, I love to teach these beginning researchers the difference between primary and secondary sources of information, as well as the difference between an archive and a museum.

Once students understand the basics, they embark on their own "heritage inquiry," visiting websites of local and regional archives, museums, historic sites, and monuments. This not only provides ample information for students to explore, question, and research, but examining the content and quality of these websites is a great learning opportunity for us all. Local used book stores often offer a bounty of resources about notable local people and events, and community resources often have experts students can interview, allowing them also to hone their interviewing skills.

The Heritage Inquiry project teaches my students communities are full of accessible resources to draw on. It's exciting to see them explore, find primary sources of information, and interact with people in their community they discover through their projects.

Teacher librarians scaffold research to nurture strong research skills.

Scaffolding research in the primary years is crucial to developing learners who have an inquiry mindset. With this in mind, we value the process of sifting and searching through nonfiction books to provide this kind of research tool even to our youngest learners. With our learners who are beginning to read or who are confident readers, at-level nonfiction texts can be used, along with various nonfiction texts found in your school or in public libraries. Nonfiction texts can be overwhelmingly inspiring and exciting, yet not at the level of the learner reading it. Teacher librarians in partnership with the classroom teacher can use tools and strategies to ensure that nonfiction text passages are a means of research for our younger learners.

Scaffolding research in the primary years is crucial to developing learners who have an inquiry mindset.

- *Reading Strategies.* Using beginner reading skills and practices, we can support learners in developing the skills they need to become strong researchers. Looking for clues in pictures to help them decipher words or understand the idea presented in the text is one of the initial strategies for young readers. This is also a powerful way for our youngest learners to use nonfiction books. Prompting learners to look at the images can lead them to answer their own questions. Then we can read the accompanying passage to them to provide more detail. This strategy encourages learners to answer their own questions and, in turn, supports them to become avid researchers!

- *Reading A to Z: Reading A to Z* is an online reading interface (https://www.readinga-z.com/) with digital and printable books. Kristen Wideen, coauthor of *Innovate with iPad*, successfully uses *Reading A to Z* to find appropriate nonfiction text passages. Kristen suggests that teachers can pre-find specific topic readings and, using Google folders, organize them by various abilities for learners to access during research blocks. For instance, if you are doing an inquiry about butterflies and have a diverse range of reading abilities in your group, *Reading A to Z* offers books on butterflies in multiple levels, allowing all of your learners to learn about butterflies while reading an appropriate text. This also opens the door to students learning different facts and then collaborating in small groups to share.

- *Research Mats.* At times we aim to take our learning deeper than we can when solely relying on images, and we recognize that reading passages out loud can be time consuming. Another way to scaffold research with our youngest learners is to use Research Mats. Research Mats are created with a specific theme or topic in mind, and QR codes link to text passages, short videos, and appropriate websites the teacher librarian has identified as grade-level appropriate or in support of a particular student's needs. Research Mats can be scaffolded to younger learners to become an independent activity using an iPad or tablet device. Create Research Mats using an 11" x 17" piece of paper and an online QR code generator (http://www.qr-code-generator.com/) to link your content to scannable codes. Save and print these QR codes onto your Research Mat along with a brief prompt of how you would like your students to interact with them or a question to keep in mind while they watch or listen. We also suggest creating a prompt or response sheet to go with the linked activities to potentially lead students to further questions and thinking about the inquiry topic or essential question.

#INQUIRYMINDSET IN ACTION

Return to trevormackenzie.com and access the free high-resolution sketchnotes from *Inquiry Mindset*. Find the "Teacher Librarian: Your Inquiry Superhero" sketchnote. Think of the teacher librarians in your world and the impact they've had on your professional growth as well as on the learning of your students. Share this sketchnote to our *#InquiryMindset* community, tag or name your amazing teacher librarian, share why they are amazing, and give them a **massive** thank you for being *your* inquiry superhero!

MAKING INQUIRY
VISIBLE

Inquiry-based learning allows learners to feel connected to their learning journey, and this process is one to be celebrated, reflected on, tweaked, and carried out. We recognize how excited and motivated students are when preparing a showcase of learning for a real audience, but we want them to feel the same level of fulfilment when sharing and reflecting on the inquiry process. The *process* is just as important—if not more so—than the final *product* of learning. Consider some of the following ideas as you work to empower your learners to feel excited and connected to their inquiry process.

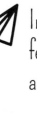

Inquiry-based learning allows learners to feel connected to their learning journey, and this process is one to be celebrated!

Pic Collage

Pic Collage is an iPad app enabling student and teacher users to create a collage of photographs of their learning process. Text, images, and stickers can be added to enhance this engaging way of capturing and documenting the inquiry process. We use the iPad to take photographs during specific activities and provocations, during the research phase or other parts of the inquiry journey. Consider prompting learners to collage images together and annotate them with memories, feelings, observations, and takeaways. Collages can be shared via digital portfolios, during family events, or with the entire class as a way to celebrate individual and group learning processes.

GoPro Footage

Purchasing a GoPro camera and a few accessories is one of the most powerful technology investments we have made to support students to make learning visible. Students have agency over checking out our class GoPro kit and wearing it as they are *in learning*, and we ask students to narrate their thoughts, actions, and processes when wearing it. We invite students to wear the GoPro when they are experimenting, designing a prototype, or practicing a new skill they're working to achieve. And students enjoy wearing the GoPro when we do an outdoor excursion or a hunt for artifacts to deepen their curiosities, wonderings, and questions. Students learn so much when they rewatch something they've experienced or have worked hard to refine; they are able to articulate their feelings and successes and to identify what they've learned. We often follow up their learning by asking students to narrate their recording to their class peers. Otherwise the footage is kept completely confidential and is only shown to parents in our digital portfolios. We love how this footage often provides a lens into the process of learning. It's powerful!

Adobe Spark

Adobe Spark turns photographs into an annotated and narrated video slideshow. Users have the option to insert photographs, icons, or images from the camera or from a safe search in the app. Audio recordings can be easily added to each image, and the app weaves your narration with your images to create a stunning slideshow, complete with a background track. Encourage students to take pictures of their research sessions, "aha moments," interesting findings, project creations, and more. They can also use Adobe Voice to document and save photographs in chronological order as they go through their inquiry journey, making it easier for them to create their video. Adobe Spark slideshows make the inquiry process visible to others *and* to your learners, who can use it to reflect on their journey. Plus, the self-assessment students experience while using Adobe Spark is impressive.

Inquiry Folders

Our learners keep their nonfiction resource books, findings, research booklets, and anything else they use for inquiry in an 11" x 17" Inquiry Folder. We encourage learners to organize their folders in the order they used the documents and made discoveries in their inquiry, and we set aside time throughout the inquiry process for them to stop and reflect. We encourage students to look through their folders and see where our inquiry began, review their initial understanding and their early wonderings, and revise and adjust if needed. We prompt students to look at how our inquiry plans may have changed and discuss any new inquiry pathways or asides leading us to exciting new research and learning opportunities. Whether our inquiry journey is unwavering in direction or explores unexpected twists of interests, wonderings, and discoveries, we celebrate and support where it takes us.

Additionally, inquiry folders are a great tool to use at any family event. Students can display their folders, and parents can see all their writing, research, and learning. Students can also use these as talking points when sharing their inquiry with their parents at student-led conferences.

Passion Boards

Passion Boards—an area in your classroom or school dedicated to sharing your learners' passions—can be a great way to make inquiry visible and honour the students' passions driving your inquiry-based learning. Try dedicating a space in your room where learners can post sticky notes highlighting what they are passionate about. Or use chart paper to create lists of what your learners love to do and post them on your classroom doors for others to see. Passion Boards create an ongoing dialogue about how passions drive our learning and how they can evolve over time. Also, remember that an inquiry teacher is forever modeling, so be sure to share your own passion as well!

Marla Margetts, Vic West Elementary School

Trevor MacKenzie, Singapore American School

Learning Documentation and Narration

Try documenting your learners' inquiry process as they go through each step in the inquiry cycle. Observe them and make anecdotal notes or take photographs of them as they dialogue, ask questions, and share their findings. Using those items, create a visual story using a poster board, a class bulletin board, or the school hallway to share the journey. As you progress, you can add students' artwork, writing, research documentation, and more. Documenting learning in this way becomes an interactive and powerful display of the inquiry process to learners, families, and your colleagues. It also allows us to reflect on the course students have taken with their learning.

Student Thinking Silhouettes

Using Student Thinking Silhouettes is an easy way to make inquiry visible! Learners create a large silhouette of their profile from an 11x17 piece of paper. We help our learners by taking a photo of their profile and projecting it onto a wall. We then tape their paper over the image so they can trace it and then cut it out. Students display the silhouettes on their desks or on a Thinking Wall in class and then cut out artifacts from magazines and newspapers and paste them into their silhouette's "brain." This allows the class to actually see what each student is thinking. Students can also add writing examples, artwork, and photographs, and they can update their silhouettes whenever they like.

Maggie Hultman, Noble Crossing Elementary

Flipgrid

We outlined Flipgrid in Chapter 7, but, since we are such big fans of this powerful platform, we wanted to touch on how it also impacts making inquiry visible. Flipgrid is intuitive and easy for students to use to share their thinking. They enjoy seeing themselves on camera, recording their thoughts and reflections, and adding emojis and symbols to their profile photos. We strengthen their learning process by providing them with accountability talk stems, like the ones that follow, prompting them to dig deeper and make more meaningful reflections.

- I agree because…
- I disagree because…
- I initially thought...because...
- My thinking changed because…
- I know this resource is helpful because…
- I learned...about my essential question.
- A new question I have is...

We can revisit these recordings to have students reflect on their learning, share with parents at Parent–Teacher Night, and even use as an assessment tool.

Immense power comes through your learners' capturing, reflecting, and sharing their *process of learning*. These tools to make learning visible not only remind students of each phase of inquiry, they also empower them to have more agency over their learning.

 Immense power comes through your learners' capturing, reflecting, and sharing their *process of learning*.

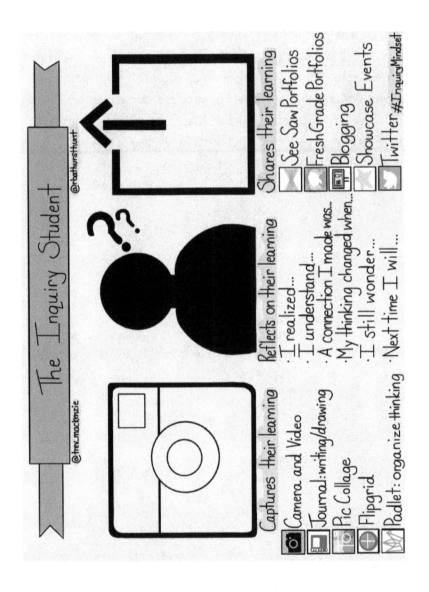

#INQUIRYMINDSET IN ACTION

Throughout this chapter, we called on you to consider the different ways and possibilities you can support your learners in **making inquiry visible**. Reflect on "The Inquiry Student" sketchnote and think on how you empower your learners to capture, reflect, and share their learning. Pick one of these three powerful processes and share to our *#InquiryMindset* community how you support your learners in capturing, reflecting, or sharing their learning. This evidence could be a photograph, an audio clip, an example of student work or reflection, a video, a Flipgrid, a Padlet, or a link to a social media post.

PUBLIC DISPLAYS OF UNDERSTANDING

When students explore topics that are genuinely meaningful to them, amazing things inevitably happen. They are engaged throughout the inquiry process, more proud of the work they do, and less anxious and concerned with the assessment of their learning. We love to maximize these benefits by sharing our inquiry with a real audience beyond the four walls of our classroom. This makes the final product of our inquiry journey meaningful, exciting, and memorable, and students are excited and motivated to prepare their showcase of learning.

> When students explore topics that are genuinely meaningful to them, amazing things inevitably happen.

When preparing a showcase of learning, we suggest keeping three things in mind: process, authenticity, and learner involvement.

Process: As we touched on earlier, the Inquiry Process is a crucial step in Free Inquiry. We love to remind our learners that the process is just as important as the final product, if not more so. However, we have found supporting our students in honouring and celebrating the process can make for an impressive showcase of learning event. We agree that the final product or showcase is special, but it must include some reflection on or capturing of their process. This invites critical reflection on what learning brought them into their final step.

Authenticity: We love to encourage our learners to keep authenticity at the core of their work. Their Free Inquiry has no doubt been a meaningful learning experience for them, and we propose that their showcase be as well. Being honest about how an inquiry process went and sharing learning and growth in an authentic and integral way trumps having the "right" answer. We avoid looking for the "right" answer; we hope learners dive into inquiry, reflect, revise, and authentically share their experiences, what they learned, and where they will go next.

Learner Involvement: Learner involvement is key when creating a showcase of learning. Students are presenting their questions, their research, their learning, and their public display of understanding so this must be *their* showcase of learning. For some teachers, letting go of a final product can be challenging; this is where learning tends to get messy, and, from the outside looking in, perhaps even chaotic. But we love this stage and encourage you to let your learners be in the driver's seat and have agency over the showcase of learning. It will be much more meaningful and authentic if you do.

As you take steps to make inquiry a powerful addition to your classroom, consider a few vehicles—*showcase events, digital portfolios,* and *blogging*—we've used to support our students in sharing their learning with an authentic audience.

SHOWCASE EVENTS

Showcases of learning involving the families of your students build excitement and empower learners to take their showcase one step further than merely sharing learning to classmates or peers at school because their family members are their number one fans. Invite families to an afternoon or evening event or to your student-led conference time. Families love interactive events, and, in our experience, attendance is amazing. Here are some of our favourite ways to create family showcases of learning:

Museum Event

Students build museum exhibits maker-style, using recycled materials, cardboard boxes, and art supplies. This is an easy way to ensure that all of the products and exhibits are student created and authentically designed by our learners. We encourage beginner writing practices and student cutting and gluing, and we enjoy seeing how proud they are of their own final products.

- We begin by brainstorming the parts of the museum we wish to include: signs, exhibits, brochures, tickets, entryway, interactive displays, and artwork, just to name a few! We often suggest that students think about their families' senses—*What will our guests look at? What will they touch? Hear? Watch?*
- We support our learners using technology to create short videos or record a science experiment. These add another engaging element to their display.
- We provide time for choice, collaboration, and design and allow for lots of building and creating time. Depending on how independent your learners are, this may be done in entire group creating time or small group creating time

during a free exploration play time. We continue to play a supportive role, encouraging and assisting where needed. We listen to what our learners need of us and from us but also step back and allow students to take an independent role in creating.

- *Pinterest* is a great tool to look up ideas for exhibit inspiration. Creating *Pinterest* boards with curated inspiration photos of projects, displays, art pieces, and exhibit setups can be a powerful way for learners to explore ideas and look for inspiration. This also allows their search to be safe and controlled because you have created the board and curated the pins.

Our museum productions—including a Weather Museum pictured here—have been successful showcase events for our students.

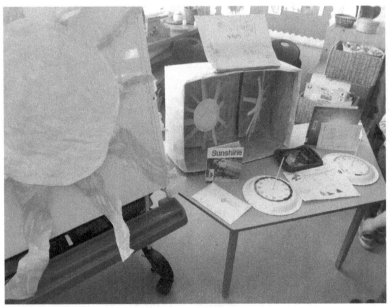

Rebecca Bathurst-Hunt, George Jay Elementary

Rebecca Bathurst-Hunt, George Jay Elementary

Rebecca Bathurst-Hunt, George Jay Elementary

Movie Theatre Event

Designing a movie theatre event can be a great way to share and celebrate digital inquiry projects that learners have created. We love for learners to dabble in creating digital pieces to showcase their learning, and we often share them via digital portfolios or class blogs. However, we have found that saving them for a special movie theatre event builds momentum and encourages learners to create more detailed and refined pieces.

- Ask your learners to brainstorm what they think they will need to set up a successful movie theatre event for their families. Items to consider could include tickets, signs, ticket booths or tables, ushers, announcers, movie trailers, popcorn, seat arrangements, and lighting. Remember to step back, allowing your learners' voices to be heard and to be the driving force of the event. Listen to what your learners need and support them in making their vision a reality.

- *iMovie* allows learners to import video footage and photographs and turn them into a movie masterpiece. Learners feel confident using *iMovie* to add music, sound effects, and text to turn their work into a real movie. It also provides a range of templates and themes to choose from if learners want to create advertisements, news broadcasts, trailers, and more!

- *Green Screen* by *Do Ink* has created a user-friendly app that allows learners to create video footage using a chosen background image or video footage. Learners can choose to share information in front of dinosaurs, underwater, or even in a moving snowstorm. They can also create artwork and talk in front of their art piece. This app is a fun and motivating way for learners to share their findings!

Schoolwide and Community Showcases

Students can share their inquiry beyond a family audience and as more than a display piece. Do you have a monthly school assembly where your students could share their learning? Could you open your class exhibit, museum, or event to other classes? We have found that students are motivated to share facts and learning with their peers and other classes.

Whole School Assembly Event

Gathering together the whole school to celebrate and hear about your class's inquiry and learning can be a positive experience for your learners. This type of showcase event allows them to share to an authentic audience beyond your classroom and create a ripple inquiry effect for other learners and your colleagues.

- Learners can choose to share orally or digitally.
- Students can share their learning and highlight pieces of their inquiry process orally, using a poster or an art piece as a speaking and visual prompt.
- Songs, poems, or dance performances are creative ways to share learning and understanding and are captivating and exciting for our young audience members.
- Adobe Spark presentations can be a powerful way to digitally celebrate your learners' inquiry process, findings from their research, and possible next steps in their learning.
- Students can dress up and play the role of experts in a *Did You Know?* presentation. Learners choose three interesting facts they learned to share with the school. Small groups of students could do this together, with some children holding up illustrations or project photographs of work or experiments they did.

- Students who aren't comfortable with or ready for *Did You Know?* might try using *ChatterPix Kids* to pick an image to "speak" for them. Students give the image a mouth, which moves while it shares an interesting fact your student has chosen. This makes the other students smile and laugh and keeps them interested in learning and listening.

Maker Faire Event

Setting up a Maker Faire can be a community-building event for your entire school. A Maker Faire is a showcase event in which maker enthusiasts gather together to share and demo their made objects, projects, crafts, and experiments. In a school setting, a Maker Faire is where students have the chance to share something they have created that is connected to their inquiry process and overall learning. Maker Faires link nicely to several activities outlined in the Four Pillars of Inquiry chapter. We enjoy watching students design and create for Maker Faires because they are motivated to create like they have never created before when the purpose is to share with the entire school.

- Support your learners with design and creation time. Ask families to send in recycled materials for a few weeks before your creation time so learners have access to a variety of supplies.
- Choose a large space at your school to set up your Maker Faire, such as your gym or library, so other classes can visit and interact with your learners. Encourage and invite other classroom teachers to sign up for a specific time or have it open during a whole afternoon, when classes can freely flow through.
- We love to invite community members to share how they are makers as well. Learners surrounded by community

makers sharing their passions and work is a very empowering experience!

DIGITAL PORTFOLIOS

Because the digital portfolio makes it easy to upload photographs, videos, and audio recordings, it is a powerful tool to create a window into the learning journey of your students. A digital portfolio can capture daily learning, inquiry processes, class events, formative assessments, and larger projects. Families are given access to their child's portfolio, creating opportunities for rich dialogue about school and learning between the child and the parent. Depending on your grade level and how comfortable you are with digital portfolios, you can involve your students in the process. Most digital portfolios are easily accessible and user-friendly for students, teachers, and parents. Consider your district's and school's stance on digital platforms, online use, and privacy etiquette to help you make informed decisions about the use of digital portfolios so they can truly empower your students in capturing and sharing their learning.

Digital portfolios make it easy to invite parents into our inquiry journey right from the start—sharing curiosities formed during provocation exploration and whole-group brainstorms or photographs and video content of topics students have posted on our Wonder Wall. We find that including parents early in this process creates powerful dialogue with families and connects learning to students' home lives. Additionally, families often jump on board and send artifacts, pamphlets, books, and other helpful resources connected to our inquiry journey. Images and video of learning *in action* are great artifacts of the inquiry process, and digital portfolios provide the vehicle for us to share these with an authentic audience.

For most parents, this is their first experience with the inquiry model, and providing a lens into the classroom proves helpful and informative. Opening the lines of communication, sharing through blurbs, photographs, and videos, and creating a window into the learning occurring in your inquiry cycle are important pieces to share with parents.

As an initial invitation to parents, we often post a description with our photographs and video to explain the emerging inquiry learning:

> *Hi families! Recently our class has been wondering about different types of weather, and we are beginning a new inquiry cycle about these and their impact on our environment and us. From our group brainstorm, you can see several types of weather interested us (see image).*
>
> *Your son or daughter will look more closely at one specific type of weather during this inquiry cycle. Students will choose the specific weather type they're interested in tomorrow and begin researching this week.*
>
> *Do you have any knowledge, resources, research tools, expertise, or equipment to help us deepen our understanding of this topic? If so, we would love for you to send them to school with your child or, better yet, come into class and share them personally.*
>
> *We are looking forward to a meaningful and exciting learning journey. Many thanks!*

This post benefits and enriches our inquiry together in the following ways:

- It provides families with a look into what we are doing in class.
- Invites families to be part of our learning by coming in and sharing or sending something to the classroom.
- Sparks child/parent discussion at home about our inquiry
- Allows parents to see the brainstorming tool we are using and their child's ideas.
- Provides the opportunity for the parents to comment on the post with ideas, comments, or suggestions.

In this way, digital portfolios can be used as a communication and update tool, but they also can be used for sharing our inquiry processes. Posting research pictures, whole-group activity shots, and process snapshots are a few great ways to share and document our learners' inquiry process.

Essentially, keeping an ongoing digital portfolio allows you to share anything learners create at any time. Traditional opportunities to send home artifacts of learning during the year come in spurts and typically at the culmination of learning or summative reflections. Using the tools of the digital portfolio allows us to "send home" so much more! We can show the process of learning as well as the end product. Plus, a digital portfolio platform makes sharing with an authentic audience simple—whether you want them to see shared videos, photographs, anecdotal reflections, or slideshows.

Using digital portfolios has also positively impacted our assessment practice. We have found that this platform strengthens our formative assessment through richly authentic feedback of student learning. By focusing on the *process* of learning as well as the *product* of learning, we have discovered that not only does student achievement increase but students' confidence and understanding of their own learning styles increase as well.

Two of our favourite online portfolio platforms are Seesaw and FreshGrade. These both have an excellent variety of options, applications, and access points to help customize and amplify sharing of learning in our classrooms.

Seesaw

Seesaw is designed so our younger students can easily use and master the platform. Children easily navigate the icons to upload images, video, notes, links, files, digital drawings, and audio clips to their portfolios, making it especially powerful for these younger learners. A helpful app function allows students to annotate photographs with both audio recordings and digital drawings to be uploaded and shared with their families. When students upload artifacts to their Seesaw journal, they are collected in an easy-to-use-and-view calendar for the teacher, keeping learning organized and easily accessible. Both teachers and students find this an intuitive and powerful platform for connecting with families.

FreshGrade

FreshGrade Teacher works as both a desktop platform and a mobile app. The online desktop platform includes access to a calendar for activities, a gradebook, each student's portfolio, and a quick add option for posting multiple photographs or learning artifacts. The teacher app allows teachers to capture learning and quickly upload on the go. Allowing you to add photos in real time, access your camera roll, and add audio clips, video clips, and notes as you go, FreshGrade is a powerfully simple digital portfolio platform. It also has a student app, creating a pathway for learners to be involved in sharing their learning process. Students can easily upload assignments, photographs, and artifacts, keeping everyone involved in the learning process and celebrating the growth that teachers see in students in every lesson.

BLOGGING TO CAPTURE LEARNING

Blogging is another vehicle that allows your students to share their inquiry process with an authentic audience. As you consider blogging, keep your learners in mind. How would they respond to the adventures of blogging? How supportive would their parents be? Can you powerfully adopt some of what we propose to impact your learning culture?

Blogging provides many benefits to our younger learners. Blogging allows us to:

- begin solidifying an understanding of digital citizenship
- share our learning to an authentic audience beyond our class and school
- develop digital fluency, including proficiency, literacy, and social competency
- become respectful and powerful contributors in the digital world

We've outlined these benefits for your consideration as well as some goals and steps for getting started using blogging to provide powerful learning opportunities for your students.

Blogging allows us to begin solidifying an understanding of digital citizenship. We propose taking a proactive approach to digital citizenship, mindfully shaping our learners' digital compasses in class each day. The teacher constantly demonstrates how to behave online in a respectful, personable, and professional manner. Our class blog is visible every day; we show our students what we post, refer to it often, and involve them in various ways. When students receive this type of modelling at a young age, they become respectful and powerful contributors in the digital world.

Blogging provides a vehicle for us to connect learning to an authentic audience. Students who grow up in a connected classroom see that their learning is more than just something handed in for marks and the teacher's eyes and thus have many advantages over other students. Blogging reinforces relevance to the world beyond the walls of our school. It can help students access expertise and understanding beyond their teacher, create and nurture rich and meaningful relationships, or impact their local and global community.

Blogging allows us to bridge the gap between home and school. Instead of weekly newsletters, try weekly blog posts to inform and connect parents to the classroom.

> Blogging provides a vehicle for us to connect learning to an authentic audience.

We suggest that you keep in mind several goals as you plan and roll out your blogging platform:

Get Started Right Away

Don't be concerned with growing an audience right away, and don't question who will read your content. Additionally, don't overthink which blogging platform to use, and don't get hung up thinking your blog has to be "picture perfect." Just get started. Blogging is a process. Over time an audience will come, people will visit your site, and you will develop and revise your online space as you see fit. You may change the appearance of your blog and tinker with the details of how it functions, but if you get caught up with this before you get started, you'll lose valuable energy, time, and potential. Get going right away, and show your learners how the space grows and changes over time. Be brave. You'll be grateful you did!

Use the Tools Available to You

We use a wide range of powerful tools to connect to our audience in engaging ways: hyperlinks to broaden understanding, images and video to bring posts to life, widgets to help create an online identity, or an array of pages to organize and direct our audience. Blogging is extremely powerful when we weave these tools into everything we publish. And when we harness the power of social media to further connect with the world outside of our classroom, this power is amplified. Whether we connect through Twitter, YouTube, Instagram, or another network, sharing to our social media outlets provides amazing opportunities for our students.

Share, Share, and Share Some More!

Sharing often and consistently is ideal. We want our learners to see the blog updated, confirming that their learning is relevant to more people than just the teacher in the room. The more we share, the more we connect with the world beyond our classroom. Set a goal for how often you want to blog, and set aside the time you need to make this goal a reality. We recommend the *20-Minute Post* approach to blogging. The goal is to write and publish your post within twenty minutes. This will keep you grounded on speaking from your heart and what you know and will create a genuine voice and personable tone. Plus, it will help ensure that blogging remains a priority and doesn't fall by the wayside in the limited time you have.

If you hope to use blogging in your classroom, it must be a manageable addition to your practice, and the *20-Minute Post* will help make this a reality.

Similar to our philosophy for adopting inquiry, we believe that introducing blogging to learners should be a scaffolded approach reflecting a gradual release of control from the teacher to the learner. We encourage teachers of kindergarten to grade three students to be the sole owner of and contributor to the blog. In other words, the teacher drafts the posts, publishes the content, and shares it with their intended audience via email, Twitter, or other professionally used social media platforms. Students are *bloggers* in the sense that they are consulted about what is to be published and prompted to provide ideas for content. At times they also contribute their learning for their teacher to post. Grades four to six students take a more active role in blogging by collaborating on posts as individuals, in pairs, or in small groups. Students submit articles to the teacher and revise based on his or her suggestions before their submission receives approval for publishing. Here the teacher is still the owner of the blog but provides more agency to the class to draft posts and publish work, similarly to how a traditional newspaper operates. Let's have a closer look at how this unfolds in our classroom.

GETTING STARTED WITH BLOGGING

Digital Citizenship and Consent

Many school districts require parental consent for their child's image to be shared online. With this in mind, at the beginning of the school year, we ensure that all parents have signed a consent form permitting us to post images of their students engaged in learning or of items they create during the inquiry journey. We believe it is important for our learners to understand what consent means to build a strong sense of digital citizenship. We don't just send the consent form home to be signed. Rather, we lead our classes through a conversation around digital rights, freedoms, and responsibilities. Having our students involved in the conversation around consent provides a powerful teaching opportunity. They learn that they need license to publish a photo of someone or an artifact created by someone else. Acquiring this understanding at a young age pays huge dividends later in schooling. Students who ask their peers for permission to post their likeness online are strong digital citizens and savvy sharers. They understand that even though they are *creating* a post, they still need the permission of everyone who is a part of its *creation*. Involving our learners in the consent conversation is a primary step toward shaping respectful online users.

If any parents or learners feel uncomfortable providing consent, we find other ways to include them in our blogging journey. At times we have posted images of learners with their face and identity not visible, either taking photos from particular angles to hide them or simply adding a smiley face emoji to cover their identity. We have a few tricks up our sleeves to ensure that everyone in our classroom can be involved.

Another reason we *love* having these consent conversations with parents is that, for the most part, parents haven't worked with educators willing to teach the nuances of digital citizenship in such a proactive manner to young students. Our conversations allow us to share our philosophy around blogging and incorporating technology in the classroom. We get to promote the benefits of blogging and our goals for our learning community. But we can also consider adapting our vision to suit the needs of our learners, based on the input and wishes of their parents.

These conversations are much more than just getting consent or approval to explore blogging together. They lay the framework for powerful conversations to occur between the educator, the learner, and the parents. When these stakeholders possess a common understanding and approach to adopting blogging, it becomes an even more powerful tool for learning.

Blogging Platforms

We've worked with a range of blogging sites we adore. Google Sites, Wordpress, Edublogs, Weebly, and Kidblog all have a similar platform in terms of flow and operation. Do a bit of research of your own to determine which of these will work best for you and your needs. Look at what your district uses at the middle and high school level and consider a platform that your students can become familiar with now and will use more in their future.

As noted previously, we are also big fans of Seesaw and FreshGrade, which also provide a rich array of digital tools to help students make learning visible to their parents and families. Many of our colleagues supplement their report cards with the content published in these digital portfolios.

We suggest you choose a single platform for all of your learners, so you have the ability to teach to the platform and troubleshoot for the entire group, and students can support one another when the opportunities arise.

BLOGGING IN THE KINDERGARTEN TO GRADE THREE CLASSROOM

For our youngest learners, the teacher is the conduit to sharing online, posting a class blog on behalf of students and with their approval. Later in their schooling, these students will take a more active role in the process, but for now, our focus is to create the foundation for blogging by sharing the vision of how we can celebrate learning online.

We want to seamlessly weave blogging and technology into our learning culture. Ideally our youngest learners will see the blog referred to in the class and at home on a consistent basis. Each day we display our blog on our class projector so our students see this learning hub where we share in the digital realm. Even if we haven't posted recently, we want the blog to be a part of our classroom environment. Blogging is our online brand, so to speak, and as such, we want it on display every day. Our students learn that blogging is another tool in their inquiry toolkit that they can use to support their learning.

For these younger students, we love publishing weekly recaps, interviews with learners, big ideas from the class, and a rundown of a field trip or school event to engage the audience and excite the classroom.

The Weekly Recap

In place of a weekly newsletter or email, use the *20-Minute Post* approach to publish something from your week that your learners found engaging. Include a brief overview of the lesson or experience to provide context for your readers, include a few photos of learning in action, and sprinkle in a personable and friendly tone. Over time, you'll discover that the parents of your students, and your PLN, will look forward to hearing what's happening in your classroom.

Interview a Learner

Post a short Q&A with a student and, with consent, share a photo of his or her smiling, adorable face. You can prepare these in advance by using this Q&A as a writing activity. Students complete the questions, and you collect them as you normally would, but make copies for your blogging use before you return them to your students. You could then post one of these every so often or do a *Learners* or *About Us* page on your blog and post these sweet bios all at once. Once your students see that they're a part of this online space, they'll feel a connection to the blog and excitement and ownership over what is shared throughout the school year.

Share a Big Idea

Every few months post a more detailed reflection from your practice to give your audience a more thorough look into the learning occurring in the classroom. At the end of a unit of study or culmination of learning, after a field trip, or as a response to a guest speaker or school event are all excellent times to share your big idea for learning and what you hoped your students would experience and glean from it. Include pictures to illustrate learning in action and add hyperlinks to demonstrate how the learning included specific resources that you used to deepen understanding. Try to compose the post clearly and with enough detail that your PLN could implement the sequence of lessons in their own practice.

Recap a Field Trip or School Event

Capitalize on your class excursions and school events by turning them into content for your blog. Take photos—or ask your learners to take photos using a class camera, iPhone, or iPod—to provide some visual context. Through a range of reflection activities once you're back in the classroom, let them tell you about their experiences and then weave their "voice" into the post. Once you publish the recap and your learners see *their* words, photos, and experience shared on the class blog, they'll feel a massive sense of accomplishment and increased engagement. Plus, they will better understand how the blog publicises their voice to a genuine audience.

BLOGGING IN THE GRADE FOUR TO SIX CLASSROOM

As our learners grow and see the powerful role of blogging and how we can responsibly use this platform to create meaningful and mindful sharing and learning experiences, we want to slowly provide them more control and agency over our blogging platform. The teacher is still the conduit to sharing online and retains control of the blog. However, at the grade four to six levels, learners begin to collaborate more with the teacher, submitting posts for approval, revision suggestions, and eventually, publication. The goal is to build on the foundation that was laid in kindergarten through grade three by continually adding blogging activities that give your growing learners a more empowered role.

Collaborate on Content

We love having learners collaborate on a post in groups of three. We typically pitch them a topic, provide them a prompt, or make a connection to learning in our room. We challenge groups to collaboratively plan, draft, revise, and polish a post to be approved for publishing. We talk about how editing teams at newspapers, magazines, and websites operate, and we watch video clips to *see* collaborative writing and publishing. As a result, students can't wait to work on their post and get their work to a quality ready to be published! We weave in brainstorming activities, editing and revising processes, and a submission step. Our learners get so excited during this "pending approval" time!

Interview an Expert

Our favourite writing activity for grade four to six learners is expert interviews. When paired with blogging, this activity doubles as a way to share learning with an authentic audience. We challenge students to interview an expert in a field they are interested in. Kids who love sports will choose an athlete or coach, kids who play an instrument will choose a musician or music teacher, and kids who love computers, gaming, and coding will choose someone in the technology sector. Learners conduct the interview, get a photo of the expert, and submit their post for approval from the teacher. The result is a series of engaging posts reflecting a high level of personal relevance from everyone in the class.

Pride Post

Learners draft a post about something they've done at school that they're proud of, and they have the creative freedom to select *anything* they'd like to write about. We ask them to include photos and, when possible, video content. Because we often discuss grit, perseverance, and growth mindset in our classrooms, learners are able to *reflect* on their learning rather than merely *summarize* an activity or lesson. The agency the Pride Post offers has amazing benefits. For example, learners always choose something they're genuinely proud of, and their feeling of accomplishment impacts the quality of their writing. Their reflections are always highly engaging, personable, and well written, therefore, providing a clear and accurate assessment for the teacher. The agency in this prompt further strengthens the empowered role students take on in the inquiry classroom—a role helping them grow into the inquisitive, creative, and innovative learners and citizens we are striving to help them become.

#INQUIRYMINDSET IN ACTION

Teachers understand how powerful sharing is in our profession. The more we share, the more we can learn from one another. This also rings true for our learners. The more we can encourage students to share their learning and connect with the broader community beyond the walls of the classroom, the more we can help them leverage the powerfully rich opportunities that arise. Please share to our *#InquiryMindset* community a photograph, a video clip, a blog link, or a portfolio example of how the amazing things in your classroom are being shared to an audience *beyond* your classroom. Your work will inspire others and encourage them to provide similar experiences of how their students are breaking down classroom walls. We can't wait to see what you share!

THE INQUIRY
ENVIRONMENT

Creating a classroom environment to foster curiosity, questioning, collaboration, and relationships helps nurture the inquiry mindset. We believe the learning space can greatly impact student creativity by encouraging students to take risks, share wonderings, and dive into inquiry with us. We want our classrooms to be welcoming, inspiring, comfortable, and thought-provoking. Keeping in mind the four learning spaces used at Anzac Park—the Cave, the Watering Hole, the Campfire, and Life (as outlined in Chapter 8)—we help our learners design spaces to support their learning needs. Simple and cost-effective changes can make a powerful impact on your learning environment!

Creating a classroom environment to foster curiosity, questioning, collaboration, and relationships helps nurture the inquiry mindset.

Seating

Consider whether your seating and table arrangement are conducive to inquiry learning. Can your learners easily collaborate, research in groups and have discussions? If not, try adjusting them into collaborative spaces such as pods, large triangles, or dinner table–style arrangements. Try adding some lower tables, trays, or coffee tables for carpet work. Having both collaborative spaces and areas for individual introspective learning is critical to allow for group work while also honouring students who wish to work independently and require quiet and isolation. We find that group tables support organic discussion and the sharing of wonderings, providing students with the ability to research and learn together. When students work in small groups, they not only learn from one another, but their conversation often naturally sparks more curiosities, leading to deeper discussions about their wonderings, our inquiry, and our collective learning. We also include a few comfy and cozy seating areas in our spaces and have experimented with lounge-style chairs, small couches, floor pillows, and floor rugs to create some alternative seating arrangements. These homelike learning areas invite students to sift through resources, research, and read informative texts.

Build and Design Your Space as You Learn

We have found that beginning the school year with a minimal amount of store-bought posters and charts on our walls is another way we can honour our learners' interests, wonderings, and ideas. We like to save wall space for their wonderings, learner-created posters or charts, and inquiry documentation. We love posting our learners' photographs and artwork around the room and having lots of space for documentation and inquiry work emerging as we learn. In our experience, the "blank canvas" fosters a welcoming environment where learners begin to quickly feel and demonstrate ownership over our learning space.

Space for Wonderings

As we described in Chapter 7, we dedicate a large area of our room to displaying student wonderings and thinking in a highly visible manner. Our Wonder Wall takes shape during our first weeks together and remains up until one of the last days of our school year, so students' thinking, learning, and curiosities are honoured all year long. We love posting large photographs of our students across an entire wall in our classroom, each one paired with a laminated thinking bubble. The photographs are beautiful, intriguing to others, and warm up our classroom. The thinking bubble allows us to write our wonderings for all to see and reuse it over and over again with new wonderings throughout the year. The Wonder Wall is a stunning dedication to amplifying learning and empowering student voice.

Provocations

Designing provocations can be a powerful way to spark interest, curiosity, and connections to curricular objectives, themes, and topics. The goal of any provocation is to provoke thought, wondering, emotion, engagement, curiosity, and questions from our learners. We also design our provocations to provide pathways for deeper inquiry.

Observation Table

One provocation method we use in our classroom is an Observation Table. We set up an area for students to observe the provocation, ask questions, and collaborate with their peers. At times objects are specifically tied to an inquiry topic or theme; other times we may use a variety of objects we believe will provoke thinking, wondering, and questions. In our experience, we've seen that, over

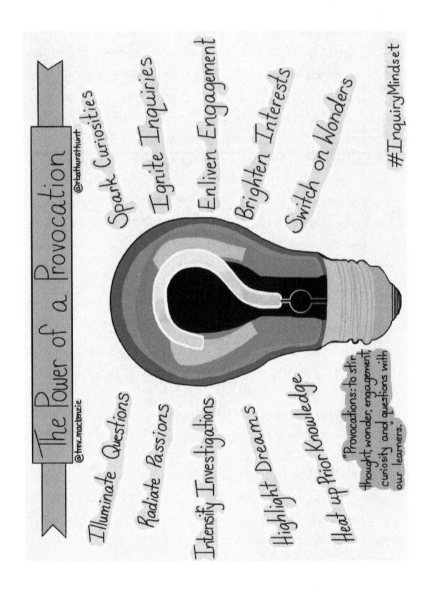

time, learners begin to bring in objects for the Observation Table and ask to construct their own display to provoke the wonderings and curiosities of their classmates. Our students and we both love the organic agency over learning in the classroom surfacing as students become artists and designers of learning experiences, potentially shaping our collective inquiry journey in class. It is powerful!

As you build your own Observation Table, you may want to consider the following:

- Use a table supporting collaboration and allowing several students to observe at any given time.
- Lay out magnifying glasses and, if possible, a large magnifying viewer for students to observe more closely what you're sharing.
- To get learners thinking and sharing, display a few prompts:
  - What do you notice?
  - What do you wonder?
  - What do you know?
  - What stories are told here?

- Provide clipboards for learners to document their observations. Have them record what they see and touch or their thoughts based on the prompts.
- Put out pencils, pens, colours, and other supplies to encourage students to capture their thoughts and provide options for adding in details when documenting their observations.
- Depending on how specific your items are, you can add a few nonfiction texts to spark further curiosity, interests, and questions. This lends extremely well to creating the initial steps into research.

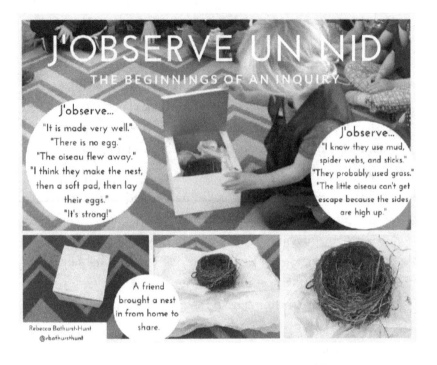

- Have a prompt attached to an iPad or tablet, encouraging learners to take pictures of what they see and capture their thinking.

We created the narrative reflection above based on what a group of learners thought when they observed a bird's nest provocation. Using Canva, a digital tool used to create narratives, posters, and brochures, we captured the wonderings and noticings of one of our younger learners.

Intriguing Items

Sharing intriguing items with the whole group is another way to provoke learning and inspire students to share their wonderings out loud. Bianca McEwen at Ecole George Jay Elementary describes a magical experience resulting from her bringing an object into her classroom to support her learners in moving from the unknown to the known:

I brought a large, rolled up strip of harvested cedar wood to my class and left it on our exploration table. My young students explored in their own way by touching, smelling, weighing, rolling, and stacking. I posed the simple yet powerful question: "What is this?" I knew most of them would not know what it was in this form. Responses varied as students piped up, "Is it a nest? Wood? A house? A wheel? A piece of the forest?"

Once I explained it was cedar, I asked the students what they wanted to know about it and how we could find the answers. We thought, shared, brainstormed, thought some more, and narrowed down a list of questions. Then we made a plan to find the answers. We asked, researched, and documented our learning, and I constantly asked students what they needed from me and encouraged them to take ownership of their learning.

They gained factual knowledge as we dove into our inquiry but, in my opinion, the magic happened when we discussed how to share the knowledge. Here we dove into why we were learning about cedar, and it provided a wonderful context and reference for deeper learning about the First People's culture in our area. The more important the students felt their knowledge was, the more they shared. I received emails from parents stating how proud their children were to educate them, their grandparents, and siblings. Seeing the excitement and pride students show when they feel confident in being both teacher and learner is incredibly rewarding.

Loose Parts

Gathering small parts from nature, home, thrift shops, and garage sales can be a great way to inspire creativity, building connection to themes, and inquiry topics. Setting loose parts around your room in accessible bins or baskets can inspire thinking and take wonderings further. Children enjoy sorting, pairing, counting, creating, and sharing curiosities about small loose parts. They are often curious about where the parts come from and why there are so many of the same thing. We suggest collecting loose parts in small collection sets. Incorporate loose parts into your play and set them up at a table and see what your students begin to create. Often younger learners will create patterns, spirals, or shapes.

As you build your own collection of loose parts, you may want to consider the following:

- Invest in a few baskets and bins for storage. Mindful placement of these items can make all the difference in what the students create.
- Consider collecting small sets of the same item, whether it be jewels, coins, nature items, straws, bottle caps, corks, stones, or whatever else comes to mind.
- Arrange the items on little mats to encourage children to build, sort, and create in a "design and build" center of sorts. This dedicated area will promote focus and help keep your classroom tidy.

- Try providing shapes (spirals, letters, numerals, etc.) for students to trace using the loose parts. This is a fantastic vehicle for creating wonderings and inquiry with literacy and numeracy roots.

Small World Area

Our Small World Area is designed to provoke wonder through *play* and *exploration.* The setting of the small world may be tied to a specific inquiry topic or theme, but it also can be more general and used to encourage curiosity about the scene's theme. Initially, we set up the area, but then we adapt it over time based on the flow of learners' interest or ideas. At times, our Small World Area has quickly evolved into something different than we ever could have imagined. We love students taking ownership over the Small World Area and leading us to unexpected and wonderful learning experiences!

Allowing space and inviting learners to create attachment, curiosity, and thinking about a specific theme or topic through play is powerful. We suggest capturing evidence of your learners' interactions with the Small World Area and how it changes based on their ideas, personalities, and interests. We take photographs, record anecdotal notes of conversations, and capture student quotes while they're interacting with the Small World Area and then share these with their families to encourage and spark meaningful conversations at home about their learning. This connects families to our inquiry and future learning experiences in the school year.

Allowing space and inviting learners to create attachment, curiosity, and thinking about a specific theme or topic through play is powerful.

As you build your own Small World Area, you may want to consider the following:

- Use a table, perhaps at kneeling height, to allow many learners to crowd around, explore, and collaborate.
- Gather pinecones, gems, corks, rocks, twigs, small tree rounds, small blocks, buttons, pompoms, or wooden beads.
- Create a Zen garden for learners to explore and play with.
- Gather artifacts such as wooden figures, felted characters, shapes, or anything tied to a specific theme you are building on in your inquiry or a theme you hope to provoke in your learners.
- If possible, provide an iPad to encourage learners to document their play. Invite children to take photographs of what they are creating and any special parts of their play and exploration. These photographs can be shared with the whole group and are a great starting point for group discussions and building interest around the theme or ideas linked with your Small World Area provocation and inquiry plans.
- Provide clipboards as an invitation to draw and document stories, wonderings, interests, and play arising during their time in the Small World Area.

Wonder Window

Another provocation we use is a Wonder Window, a specific area at one of our windows to encourage outdoor observations and wonderings. Using tape, we frame an area on the glass to encourage our learners to look out and share what they see. We open our curtains and blinds, build from our outdoor activities throughout the weeks, and recognize and celebrate changes in the natural world around us.

When we notice action outside, we use it as an opportunity to hone our inquiry mindset. If there is a machine digger working across the street from our class, we open our blinds and encourage our students to draw what is happening. If there is a lawnmower cutting the grass of our school field, we prompt our learners to capture their observations. When the weather changes and it begins to rain or starts to snow or the sun pokes out from behind the clouds, we keep our blinds open and invite children to orally express what they are noticing and prompt them to question and share why they think the weather is changing. Having a specific area for gazing and observing can be a great way of prompting natural wonderings and explorations.

As you build your own Wonder Window, you may want to consider the following:

- Tape around a window or empty picture frame. If possible create a frame resembling an ornate art, picture, or portrait frame. This creates a museum-like atmosphere!
- If possible, supply a few sets of inexpensive binoculars or magnifying glasses to prompt looking more deeply through the Wonder Window.
- Create a Wonder Journal, provide clipboards, or supply paper and writing utensils to prompt documentation of observations.
- If possible, provide an iPad for students to capture photographs. We pair student images with Adobe Spark so learners can take a photograph and then record their observations and put voice to what they see. This can then be shared with the entire class or in our digital portfolio platform with their families.
- Pair the Wonder Window with a small collection of books to spark interest in outdoor activity and environmental changes.

As you can see, you can easily rethink and redesign your class-room environment to provoke student curiosities, wonderings, and questions. Any teacher—even one on a tight budget—can take on these suggestions and empower their learners in inquiry.

#INQUIRYMINDSET IN ACTION

In this chapter, we propose a variety of manageable and mean-ingful ways you can change your learning environment to best support inquiry. Spend a few minutes alone in your classroom and observe the design of your space. Where would you like to shift, rear-range, redesign, or restructure something based on what we propose in this chapter? Once you've identified a specific area or feature that you would like to transform, take a few photos of the space before you move forward with your plans. Once you've documented the space, go ahead and put into action the changes you've identified that will help empower your students in inquiry. Again, capture your hard work as you're implementing your plan and capture the process of your redesign and the changes you're making. Finally, once your redesign is complete, take some photos of your new space. Share the most poignant images with our *#InquiryMindset* community so we can all see your inviting space and learn more about the transforma-tion you created!

INQUIRY AND
INCLUSIVE EDUCATION

Whether students are well fed and loved or impoverished and neglected, intellectually capable or facing particular challenges in their learning, all learners can thrive in inquiry. A common myth about inquiry is that student agency and empowerment is only for particular students. However, all of our learners not only *deserve* the opportunity to shape their learning pathways, but they can be incredibly successful when given the understanding, skills, and mindset to do so.

All learners not only *deserve* the opportunity to shape their learning pathways, but they can be incredibly successful when given the understanding, skills, and mindset to do so.

This is especially true with our students with diverse learning needs. As noted throughout *Inquiry Mindset* and *Dive into Inquiry*, we have witnessed how an inquiry approach empowers students when they understand their learning strengths and needs. When relevance, authenticity, and agency are woven into the classroom, students are more engaged in their learning, more willing to dig deeper, and persevere through the ups and downs of learning. Additionally, they are more competent communicators and collaborators.

With this in mind, we'd like to outline a few big ideas to help you successfully adopt inquiry with your students with diverse learning needs.

INCLUSIVE EDUCATION

We propose when rolling out inquiry with our students who have diverse learning needs that you begin with creating an inclusive-education classroom and school community. Inclusive education means that all learners attend and are welcomed at their neighborhood school in age-appropriate, regular classes, and are supported to learn, contribute, and participate in all aspects of the school. Students with diverse learning needs do not attend a different school or program pulling them away from their friends or peer group. Rather the goal is to have all students, despite their learning abilities, learn in the same classroom with support provided where needed.

All students learning in an inclusive environment benefit from the diversity in the room. As students learn their individual strengths and set personalized learning goals, they also become aware of their own specific challenges and the support resources available to them. Furthermore, inclusive education fosters a classroom and school culture of respect as students form friendships and collaborations with a wide array of children, each unique in their abilities and challenges.

Inquiry thrives in the inclusive education environment. When trust and relationship are at the forefront of learning, every student benefits from the others. If students work with a specialist or resource teacher *outside of class*, they are withdrawn from the trust of and relationship with their peers and inquiry teacher, and the powerful impact of agency is stripped away. Too often we have witnessed these learners, under the best intentions of the professionals involved, being ostracized and labeled because they are pulled out of class. Their sense of self is scarred.

Inclusive-education classes invite support personnel to enter the inquiry classroom and work with specific students alongside their peers and in our learning community. This provides some natural and powerful opportunities for all students to collaborate, support, and grow together.

Inclusive-education classes invite support personnel to enter the inquiry classroom and work with specific students alongside their peers and in our learning community.

UNIVERSAL DESIGN FOR LEARNING

We are big fans of *Universal Design for Learning (UDL)*, a framework for curriculum planning that provides the following:

- *Multiple means of representation,* to give learners various ways of acquiring information and knowledge
- *Multiple means of expression,* to provide learners with alternatives for demonstrating what they know
- *Multiple means of engagement,* to tap into learners' interests, challenge them appropriately, and motivate them to learn

We believe that everything we propose in *Inquiry Mindset* and *Dive into Inquiry* supports these tenets of UDL, outlining how, in the inquiry classroom, students are empowered to gain understanding from a variety of sources and demonstrate their understanding in a variety of ways while exploring their interests, curiosities, and passions. Fundamental to the UDL framework is the belief that the pedagogical design is best for *everyone* in the inquiry classroom. Creating personalized learning pathways through inquiry follows this design. It provides the process and structures to best support all of your learners. All learners can ask a question as their starting point to inquiry, and this beginning of learning—with an essential question, wondering, or curiosity—shapes the student experience in the inclusive-education classroom.

All learners can ask a question as their starting point to inquiry, and this beginning of learning—with an essential question, wondering, or curiosity— shapes the student experience in the inclusive-education classroom.

INDIVIDUALIZED EDUCATION PLANS

In the inquiry classroom, students with individualized education plans (IEPs) are involved in the process of building and maintaining their learning pathway, identifying supports needed, and reflecting on and revising this plan throughout the year. These students actually *know* their IEP. So often the IEP is merely created by a case manager or teacher and signed off by a parent, and the student never sees it. In the inquiry classroom, our students' role in this process is quite different. We honour their voices by allowing them agency in the process of structuring their learning pathways and IEPs.

When learners are given agency and responsibility over their learning, they know what their strengths and needs are. They understand how programming is modified or accommodated for them, the instructional strategies applied for them, assistive technology available to them, and the environmental accommodations they have access to. Inquiry empowers our learners to have ownership over their IEPs.

DIFFERENTIATION

Opportunities for true differentiation—teachers working beside a student who requires support and care—occur often in the inquiry classroom, for a number of reasons. First, collaboration and grouping are facets of inquiry enhancing differentiation. Whether in Controlled Inquiry, in which students are exploring the same essential question, in Guided Inquiry, in which students are working in groups on the same topic and sharing ideas and resources, or in Free Inquiry, in which students have chosen a similar wondering or learning pathway, opportunities to differentiate are plentiful.

Second, when students are genuinely exploring topics of personal relevance and in authentic ways, the inquiry teacher can be more fluid in his or her use of time in class. Rather than lecturing at the front of the room, the inquiry teacher can join students *in learning* and can work to differentiate *in the moment*, based on his or her observations of the needs of each specific student.

> Rather than lecturing at the front of the room, the inquiry teacher can join students *in learning* and work to differentiate *in the moment*, based on their observations of the needs of each specific student.

And finally, when students are empowered and understand their strengths and challenges, over time they begin to differentiate *for themselves*. Whether by selecting a video over text to deepen understanding, an interview over an artifact to research an inquiry topic, or a presentation over a sample of writing to demonstrate understanding, when students know what works for their learning, they begin to differentiate to best support themselves. Powerful!

SETTING UP THE CONDITIONS FOR LEARNING

Beginning inquiry in inclusive-education classes and programs starts with setting up the conditions for learning. This is much different at the elementary school level from the high school setting because a single teacher works with a group of elementary students for most of the school day. Because there is less movement between classrooms, teachers, and pedagogical frameworks, the elementary school structure presents some amazing opportunities for inquiry and personalized learning. Individual teachers can plan across longer blocks of time, depending on where inquiry learners are. Integration of traditional disciplines occurs as an essential question is rooted in a specific subject, but it will likely touch on several other areas throughout our inquiry unit. Additionally, there are more opportunities for collaboration and team teaching, and deepening learning outside the classroom and in the community is easier. Clearly, inquiry is powerfully supported at the elementary level because it is literally built into the school's framework!

In our inclusive-education classes, all students develop an idea of who they are as learners throughout the year. They develop an awareness, not only of their own strengths and needs as a learner, but of other learners' strengths and needs as well. A true learning community forms, one in which collaboration is natural, and soft skills and competencies are nurtured.

#INQUIRYMINDSET IN ACTION

In this chapter, we outlined the power that inquiry can bring for *all of our learners.* Throughout our careers, we have witnessed how inquiry creates meaningful and relevant learning opportunities for some of our most vulnerable students, those with diverse learning needs. In what ways has inquiry helped you to include all of your learners? Share one celebration of how you differentiated and personalized to better meet the needs of one of your students. Share your artifact of this celebration with our *#InquiryMindset* community.

CONCLUSION

At the onset of *Inquiry Mindset,* we described the inquiry teacher and some of the understandings, characteristics, and values these educators possess. We challenged you to embark on your reading of this book with a professional growth plan in mind—being mindful of your goals as a teacher, reflecting on your practice, and doing everything possible to better meet the needs of your learners. Appropriately, we framed your reading with an essential question:

After reading *Inquiry Mindset,* how will you enter the classroom a different and more complete teacher than ever before?

Now is the time to put into action everything you feel will make this dream a reality.

To support you in your journey beyond *Inquiry Mindset,* we invite you to continue to document your growth, your adoption of inquiry into your practice, and the impact this journey has on your learners to our *#InquiryMindset* community. You are one of countless educators around the globe asking the same question: *How can I better meet the needs of my learners?* Let's rely on one another, support each other, and continue, as always, to learn from one another.

All the best in your inquiry journey.

We'll see you soon.

Trevor   Rebecca

ACKNOWLEDGMENTS

From Trevor

To my lovely wife Sarah: unceasingly supportive, endlessly giving, and always leading with your heart. I owe ya. To my sons, Ewan and Gregor: You guys rock! I thank you for the joy you bring to our world each and every day. You continue to open my eyes to all that is important in life: being in the moment, warm embraces and cuddles, family, and above all else, love. To my family, friends, and colleagues who have been a part of this beautiful life, my deepest thanks. And to my mum, Marlene. Finishing this book would never have happened without your endless love and support. You have taught me so much. I know that wherever you are, you are proud of me. I love you.

From Rebecca

A huge thank you to my number one supporters: my partner Philip, my parents, Elaine and Clive, and my brother, Freddie—I love you all. Your love and energy keeps me fueled, grounded, and passionate. You continue to remind me to do my best and to take big leaps. To my friends and colleagues, especially at George Jay Elementary School, thank you for your continuous love and for always keeping me laughing.

From Us Both

To Holly Clark for her vision, her dedication, and her support. We cannot thank you enough! To Erin Casey and her talented editing and design team—we are grateful to have had your expertise working with us through this amazing journey! Hugs and love to our critical friends who lent their voice, guidance, and support in making this book what it is: Petra Eggert, Maggie Hultman, Austin Kjorven, Marla Margetts, Bianca McEwen, Nadine McIntyre, Sarah McLeod, Kelli Meredith, Kath Murdoch, Lorraine Powell, Dave Shortreed, and Jane Spies. And to the families who share their learners with us each and every day, we are forever grateful.

BIBLIOGRAPHY

Focus on Inquiry: A teacher's guide to implementing inquiry-based learning. Edmonton: Alberta Learning, 2004. open. alberta.ca/dataset/032c67af-325c-4039-a0f3-100f44306910/ resource/b7585634-fabe-4488-a836-af22f1cbab2a/ download/29065832004focusoninquiry.pdf.

Kaufman, Josh. "The First 20 Hours: How to Learn Anything." YouTube Video. 19:27. March 14, 2013. Retrieved from: youtube.com/watch?v=5MgBikgcWnY

McTighe, Jay, and Grant Wiggins. Understanding by Design. Alexandria, VA: Association for Supervision and Curriculum Development, 2005.

Murdoch, Kath. The Power of Inquiry: Teaching and learning with curiosity, creativity and purpose in the contemporary classroom. Melbourne, Australia: Seastar Education, 2015.

Rose, David H., Anne Meyer, Nicole Strangman, & Gabrielle Rappolt. Teaching Every Student in the Digital Age: Universal Design for Learning. Alexandria, VA: ASCD, 2002.

Rothstein, Dan, and Luz Santana. Make Just One Change: Teach Students to Ask Their Own Questions. Cambridge, MA: Harvard Education Press, 2011.

Thornburg, David D. Campfires in Cyberspace: Primordial Metaphors for Learning in the 21st Century. Lake Barrington, IL: Thornburg Centre, 2007. nsd.org/cms/lib/WA01918953/Centricity/ Domain/87/TLC%20Documents/Other%20TLC%20Documents/ CampfiresInCyberspace.pdf.

"What Is Inclusive Education?" InclusionBC. Accessed October 15, 2017. inclusionbc.org/our-priority-areas/inclusive-education/ what-inclusive-education.

Wideen, Karen. Innovate with iPad: Lessons to Transform Learning. Irvine, CA: EdTechTeam Press, 2016.

BRING MEANINGFUL AND HIGH ENERGY PD TO YOUR SCHOOL, DISTRICT OR EVENT.

Inquiry Mindset workshops are designed to bring inquiry to your students, staff, and school through a scaffolded and intentional process.

We facilitate how inquiry looks, feels, and sounds using examples from our classrooms to deepen your understand and create context and capacity.

We customize the day to fit the needs of your school or district, and provide support and structure for you to positively impact your students.

This masterclass will be built around action. Teachers will leave the day with inquiry plans that are ready to roll out immediately. The day will be built around the doing of inquiry and as such attendees will feel inspired as well as informed.

The workshop will include a look at:
- Creating a culture of inquiry
- Building trust & relationship in the classroom
- Formative assessment to empower learners
- Igniting interest, wonder, and curiosity in our curriculum
- Scaffolded and intentional inquiry steps
- The Question Formulation Technique

To inquire regarding speaking engagements for Trevor, fill out the form at **trevormackenzie.com/contact** or for Rebecca, email **rbathurst@sd61learn.ca**.

MORE BOOKS FROM

ELEVATEBOOKSEDU.COM

Dive into Inquiry
Amplify Learning and Empower Student Voice

By Trevor MacKenzie

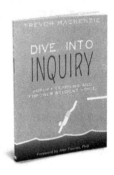

Dive into Inquiry beautifully marries the voice and choice of inquiry with the structure and support required to optimize learning. With *Dive into Inquiry* you'll gain an understanding of how to best support your learners as they shift from a traditional learning model into the inquiry classroom where student agency is fostered and celebrated each and every day.

The Google Infused Classroom
A Guidebook to Making Thinking Visible and Amplifying Student Voice

By Holly Clark and Tanya Avrith

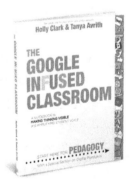

This beautifully designed book offers guidance on using technology to design instruction that allows students to show their thinking, demonstrate their learning, and share their work (and voices!) with authentic audiences. The Google Infused Classroom will equip you to empower your students to use technology in meaningful ways that prepare them for the future.

Sketchnotes for Educators
100 Inspiring Illustrations for
Lifelong Learners

By Sylvia Duckworth

Sketchnotes for Educators contains 100 of Sylvia Duckworth's most popular sketchnotes, with links to the original downloads that can be used in class or shared with colleagues. Interspersed throughout the book are reflections from Sylvia about what motivated her to create the drawings as well as commentary from many of the educators whose work inspired her sketchnotes.

How to Sketchnote
A Step-by-Step Manual for Teachers
and Students

By Sylvia Duckworth

In this fun and inviting book, Sylvia equips you with the basic tools you and your students need to introduce doodling and sketchnoting in the classroom. With step-by-step sketchnote practice sessions and 180+ icons you can use or adapt to represent your ideas, *How to Sketchnote* will inspire you to embrace the doodler within—even if you think you can't draw.

About the Authors

Trevor MacKenzie is an award winning English teacher at Oak Bay High School in Victoria, BC, Canada, who believes that it is a magical time to be an educator. By increasing student agency over learning, weaving in strong pedagogy, transformative tech use, and sharing learning to a public audience, Trevor's learners are ready to take on important roles in the 21st century.

Trevor is the author of *Dive into Inquiry: Amplify Learning and Empower Student Voice* as well as *Inquiry Mindset: Nurturing the Dreams, Wonders and Curiosities of our Youngest Learners* (co-authored with Rebecca Bathurst-Hunt) published by Elevate Books Edu.

Connect with Trevor

 Blog: trevormackenzie.com

 @trev_mackenzie

 trevormackenzie.com/contact

Rebecca Bathurst-Hunt is a French Immersion Kindergarten teacher in Victoria, BC, Canada. She is passionate about empowering learners to ask deep questions that are connected to their interests and passions. She builds off learners' curiosities  and wonders to help support them in developing an Inquiry Mindset. Rebecca is a thoughtful sketchnote artist and an enthusiastic blogger in the education community.

Rebecca co-authored *Inquiry Mindset: Nurturing the Dreams, Wonders, and Curiosities of our Youngest Learners* with Trevor Mackenzie published by Elevate Books Edu.

Connect with Rebecca

 Blog: rebeccabathursthunt.com

 @rbathursthunt

 rbathurst@sd61learn.ca